Grantseeking Primer
for
Classroom Leaders

Grantseeking Primer for Classroom Leaders

David G. Bauer

New York • Toronto • London • Auckland • Sydney

ISBN 0-590-49216-0

12 11 10 9 8 7 6 5 4 3 2 1   4 5/9

Printed in the U.S.A.

Library of Congress Cataloging-in-Publication Data

Bauer, David G.
    Grantseeking primer for classroom leaders/David G. Bauer.
    p. cm.
    Includes bibliographical references. (p.125).
    1. Educational fund-raising. 2. Proposal writing in education. 3. Proposal writing for grants. I. Title.
LC241.B38 7   1993   92–39715
379.1'3—dc20   CIP

Designed by Joan Gazdik Gillner

Contents

Acknowledgments

The individuals truly responsible for the creation of this primer are those teachers who worked so hard to take a rebellious and troublesome youth and instill in him a love for teaching. I dedicate this book to the teachers in New York Mills Public High School who did not throw me out of class but allowed me to assist them in teaching parts of the curriculum to elementary and junior high school students. They creatively channeled my interests and energy — the same energy that could easily have been used to create chaos in the classroom.

I also acknowledge with gratitude the encouragement and hard work of my partner and associate, Donna Macrini Bauer. My early teachers and wife have helped me become a better teacher and writer than I would or could have become on my own.

Introduction

Successful grantseeking is one of the foremost vehicles for developing, enhancing, and delivering your classroom's educational programs. Seeking grant funds for elementary and middle school education is in itself a positive process because the need flows from a desire to implement a proposed project, change or develop a program, procure equipment, or, in some cases, evaluate or perform research that will benefit education. However, seeking grants solely for the sake of bringing money into a school can result in confusion and rapid, erratic changes in your educational focus. Money, be it grant funds or any other, does not ensure that education will be advanced. Increased funding for education does not guarantee improved educational experiences or learning outcomes. Educators, administrators, and taxpayers are aware that increasing school budgets and raising taxes to support education do not necessarily mean that educational programs will be improved, that parents and the community will become involved, or that children will learn. But if an educator is willing to make the effort to work with a community advisory committee to develop a grant proposal, participants are more likely to use the resources resulting from their hard work to effect change and improve the educational atmosphere. Use the grantseeking techniques presented in this primer and you will enhance your educational programs. You will also be rewarded with:

- solutions to your school's problems,
- an increase in school/community involvement,
- more successful ways to use volunteers, and
- an increase in the number of parents and children involved in the development and use of educational resources.

Most of the people in my age group (45 to 50) who have been involved in education for twenty years or more are skeptical of individuals, groups, or programs that espouse educational change that is unaccompanied by an increase in funds to support new and improved programs. We have witnessed many innovations that demonstrated positive educational outcomes. But because the funds subsidized only a model project, not the program's operation or replication, the program never materialized. While money and resources alone do not ensure a great educational program, they are the basis for sustained change and improvement once a program is proven worthwhile. Parents and school administrators must realize that grant monies increase the rate of educational improvement. Carrying on valid educational improvements and making them available to more students should be the work of taxes and levies, not increased grantseeking. Your school district must realize that some of the programs started with grant monies will require other forms of support once the grant is completed and the methodology proven worthwhile.

It is important to note the difference here between grantseeking and fund-raising. Grantseeking is one way of raising funds. A proposal for a grant is an outline of an agreement to address a particular situation by means of prescribed steps. Fund-raising uses a variety of techniques to encourage donors to give money to an organization and a cause. Money gained from fund-raising can be used for the general support of a school's mission. Almost anything that enhances education can be supported by monies raised in a general fund-raising appeal. However, grantseeking is based on prescribed activities that are supposed to bring about results in a specific area of education. For example, educators are forced to seek grant funds for materials and equipment that are impossible to obtain through budgets or other general fund-development sources (e.g., parent-teacher groups, and so on). Grantseeking provides an answer to the problem of resource development in our nation's elementary and middle schools, but it is difficult if not inappropriate to use grants for the continuation of programs.

By reading this primer, you will learn how and when to employ the grants mechanism to get funds to help you reach your classroom's educational goals and objectives, acquire materials and equipment, and move your school in the direction you want.

It is best when your educational system, whether it consists of one site or an entire district, is willing to support your grants effort. But your school district must realize that some of the programs started with grant monies will require other forms of support once the grant is completed and the methodology proven worthwhile.

Too many school systems encourage classroom leaders to invest their out-of-school and spare time to pursue grants and then get cold feet when they are asked for matching funds and in-kind contributions or are shown a formula to increase the school's commitment to the project over a given period of time. Even when the proposal seems simple and the benefits obvious — such as getting a grant for five new classroom computers — issues such as who pays for the software, maintenance, and storage need to be addressed before the proposal is submitted and the hardware arrives. The old adage "You don't get something for nothing" rings true in the educational grants arena, too. Gifts and grants have many hidden costs that need to be addressed in advance of proposal submission.

This primer describes grantseeking techniques that will increase your chances for success and provides you with a time-efficient proposal development system. As a former middle school teacher, I know firsthand the pressures and demands on the educator's time. Therefore, I also know that before you invest your valuable time in a grantseeking venture, you must know what works.

The key to implementing my systematic approach to grantseeking is understanding that the process parallels the development of superior educational achievement and is based on the school community's involvement. From developing fundable ideas to incorporating an information system that ascertains who can help us get our foot in the door with a funding source, the system works because of the commitment and involvement of volunteers — be they parents, friends of education, graduates, or even students themselves.

This grants primer provides you, the classroom leader, with a time-efficient method that helps you mobilize your resources to:

- organize your proposal ideas,
- write a cogent and effective proposal,
- obtain grant funds, and
- experience the fun and excitement of implementing your proposal.

The formula for grants success is:

FORMULA FOR SUCCESSFUL GRANTSEEKING

Needs	+	**Solutions**	+	**Commitment**	=	**Educational Advancement**
of your students, classroom, community, and society		ideas and strategies to adapt change, strengthen the educational system		the extra effort of you, your colleagues, and parents	∞ *	New strategies, equipment, and materials to meet the challenges of education

*Grantseeking provides the catalyst in this equation. Change occurs at an increased rate.

Remember that grant money is not the end, nor is it the beginning of a quest. It is the catalyst in the formula. In fact, when a grants system is set up properly, it will lead to positive outcomes even without that catalyst. When an idea-generating and problem-solving system is developed with positive outcomes as the desired result, the classroom, school, and community will move in that positive direction. However, progress will be slow if the catalyst, money, is not there. In contrast, school communities that continually focus on what is wrong (i.e., what they don't have) stagnate, or even deteriorate and find it difficult to generate excitement about their projects.

Some educators believe that money alone is the answer and that an increase in resources will solve education's problems. However, having more catalyst than necessary does not increase the speed or strength of the reaction or produce the desired results. The proper equation needs balance — balance that can occur only when the correct amount of each component is used.

You, the classroom leader, control the chemistry and must keep the balance of the equation in mind. A grants system can depend too much on the supervisor and/or administration. Quality ideas and educational solutions spring from an environment that questions what works, why it works, and how to make it work better. It takes parents, teachers, school staff, and a supportive administration to make a grants effort succeed, but the classroom leader is the basic element.

Novice grantseekers mistakenly assume that the school should provide someone to write their ideas into a proposal. That approach seldom works. You probably do not need or want anyone else to write your proposal, but you may need internal support services. Contact your district office and supervisor to determine what assistance the district can provide and to ensure that you follow all district procedures and rules.

Scholastic Inc. and Bauer Associates have produced a guide for grants success for principals and another for central office district administrators. Both of these contain suggestions for how these individuals in their respective areas of responsibility can provide valuable assistance to you, the classroom teacher.

One danger in grantseeking that you should be aware of is that if you write many successful proposals and promote more programs than your students and school/community can assimilate, you may end up as I did:

- removed from the classroom,

- given the difficult task of helping others achieve grants success on a full-time basis, and

- enjoying the excitement, challenge, and rewards that the grants process brings to your school, students, colleagues, and communities.

Resource development is a very potent force in education. In fact, you may be able to effect a positive influence on more students than just those in your classroom by using your skills, this primer, and your successful example to help others find — and win — grants. Although I developed my grant-winning techniques over a span of twenty years, I started with my classroom. Then I was asked to help my colleagues, then my district, and finally an entire intermediate district. I know these techniques will work, but only you control the real key to your grants success — your desire to bring about positive change in the classroom.

Bauer Associates supplies several valuable products and services created to support your grantseeking efforts. For a price list of our ancillary material, or to discuss the possibility of having David Bauer conduct a grants training seminar for your school or district, phone 1–800–836–0732.

CHAPTER ONE

Why Write Grant Proposals?

Why do teachers become involved in grantseeking? It is not in their job description, and in many cases their efforts may earn them nothing at all in the way of extra money. So why get involved? For more than 20 years I have asked myself and hundreds of educators from the elementary through the postgraduate level this very question. The answers fall into three major categories. Educators write grant proposals to:

1. improve teaching (change or supplement the curriculum, obtain new materials, and acquire equipment by means other than district-supported funds);
2. improve the school-community educational support system (increase parent and volunteer participation and further involve the community in the education of its youth);
3. obtain the feelings of self-esteem that come with managing a funded project (controlling a budget; knowing that you make a difference; asking and answering questions about education and thus expanding the universe of knowledge about how students learn).

You do not need to have a doctorate in education or be a statistical wizard or evaluation-design genius to become involved in grantseeking. Armed with your interest in education, your classroom and students, your motivation, and the step-by-step techniques outlined in this book, you *can* attract grant money.

In my case, I was a health teacher whose students needed information and skills to help them deal with their problems. One of my first funded projects was to develop a program to improve nutritional choices for elementary school children. After the project was completed, I was invited to present my results at a national conference, with travel expenses provided by the grant. Not only was my program a success but I also had the enjoyment of traveling, gaining recognition from my peers, and building my feeling of self-worth. All this can be yours too when you *succeed* at grantseeking!

Demystifying The Grants Process

Many classroom leaders do not become involved in grantseeking because they think the process is a mystery or that it requires a support staff of professionals and a tremendous investment of time. Neither could be further from the truth. While a school grants coordinator can play a valuable role in grantseeking, you, the educator, drive the system. If you want the resources that grantseeking can provide, your initiative and the techniques outlined in this primer will guide you to grants success. As your administration seeks to replicate your success, your district will supplement the existing grants system or begin to develop one. But don't wait for the school administrator to act first. You can start now!

This primer is one of three books in the Scholastic/Bauer Grants Series. The other two are *The Principal's Guide to Grants Success* and *Successful Grants Program Management.* Developed for principals and district administrators respectively, both guides reaffirm these individuals' importance in developing your grants effort. But remember, you cannot be replaced in the process. You are the generator of ideas, the initiator, and the implementer. It all starts with you and takes place in your classroom and community.

While most school systems have a central grants office that prepares and often coordinates or administers grants, this office traditionally focuses on laying the groundwork for the district's federal grants efforts. These grants, usually known as Title Grants, refer to the entitlement programs that fall under the federal government's Elementary and Secondary School Act. In many cases, the types of innovations allowed under these programs are limited, and the guidelines are quite specific. However, your input into these proposals may be an avenue that you should explore with your central office personnel. By making an effort to understand your grants system you may also get help with budget development, locating potential funding sources, proposal requirements, sign-off procedures, and/or other formalities that could slow you up when it comes time to submit your proposal. Check with your district's grants office first. But regardless of your district's support, this primer will take you *beyond* the grants that are based on entitlements and formulas to the billions of dollars in grants that are available for proposals that *you write* for programs (projects, equipment, and so on) for *your classroom.*

Obviously, you want to avoid the common pitfalls of the rejected grantseeker, increase your chances of success, and use the time you invest in grantseeking to its fullest. If you ask a foundation or corporate funding source to name the most common and fatal mistakes grantseekers make, they will list many of the same problems they would have listed 20 years ago. Every year they receive piles of poorly prepared, hastily written proposals. How can you capitalize on this history of errors to develop a successful proposal? Learn what the most common mistakes are and review *Bauer's Rules of Proposal Development.*

Rule 1 — A successful grants system takes work. A large percentage of the 15,000 individuals I have instructed in my grants seminars received one grant before attending. In fact, often their successful grant was a result of their first attempt at proposal development. However, after that initial success, they received a number of rejections. They came to my seminar to learn why they never struck gold again. Basically, it's because they were just lucky in their first attempt. As in other professions, homework, hard work, and practice are the keys to consistent grants success, *not luck.* (No one knows better the benefits of doing homework than we who assign it.) This primer will provide you with shortcuts, tips, and time-saving grants strategies, but *you* must add the *work* that will turn them into a successful system.

Rule 2 — Funders don't care what you need or want to do. Be it curricular reform or new equipment, no funding source cares about what you want in exactly the same way you do or sees the same results or benefits in your project as you do. Grantors have *their own reasons* for funding projects. Grantors fund recipients because they see or think they see benefits or results that they value. First-time recipients especially may not even be aware of grantors' reasons for funding them or of the funding sources' expectations. The message here is that if you do not have a clear picture of the benefits that your grantor expects, you may highlight the wrong data and examples in your reporting and evaluation and have difficulty obtaining subsequent funding.

Rule 3 — Better to send your proposal to one funding source and be awarded than to 100 funding sources and be rejected. This rule has several components.

a.) **The "shotgun" approach to grantseeking repulses grantors.** Just as you dislike "Dear Occupant" junk mail, most funders dislike receiving a proposal that has been submitted to several other potential funding sources. This "shotgun" approach is like haphazard bird hunting. If you shoot enough bullets in the air, an unsuspecting and unlucky bird may eventually fly into one of them. However, funding sources are much smarter than birds, and this type of grantseeking actually insults the potential funding source. While a direct-mail appeal may motivate some to make individual donations, there is a great difference between a $20 individual contribution and a $20,000 grant award. Grant funders expect a tailored and individualized appeal that acknowledges their value to the field of education and to children.

b.)Rejection means negative positioning, and funding sources have long-term memories. In marketing terms, the name recognition of your school is its "positioning value," and in the grants arena you do not get credit for trying and failing.

A 1 percent success rate means that 99 times out of 100 the funding source not only rejects your proposal but also has solid evidence that you do not do your homework. For example, your proposal may indicate to them that you do not know what types of projects they fund, their average grant size, or the types of institutions or organizations to whom they prefer to fund. Funding sources want to work with winners. You should aim at a grants success rate of 25 percent to 50 percent. To succeed 50 percent of the time, *do your homework!* Know which funders to go to, why they would want to fund you, and for what amount of money.

Rule 4 — Whom you know is more important than what you know. As a classroom teacher, I thought that you needed to be a superintendent of schools or a politician to need to keep track of whom you knew who could influence the outcome of a grants competition. Since then, I have learned that whom you know *can* influence the outcome of a grants competition and that individuals tend to know far more people than they think. Whom you know and whom the people that you know can get in touch with are worth their weight in gold.

One of my students was the nephew of the mayor of the city I taught in. While not a major metropolis, its population was 80,000. It had mayoral advisory committees and funding for grants in literacy, vocational education, substance abuse, and a variety of other areas. Thanks to a common bond between me and the mayor (i.e., his nephew, my student), I was named to several of the mayor's committees and helped these groups see the wisdom of funding public elementary and junior high school educational programs to prevent problems.

In short, you must get involved and keep track of who could help you get corporate, foundation, and government grants. (More on this to come.)

Rule 5 — Quality proposals do not float to the top like cream on milk — they are pushed up there. After you read this primer and understand how funding sources view the world and how few staff they have to help them separate the excellent proposals from the good ones, you will feel justified in using every possible advantage to ensure that your proposal gets the attention it and your students deserve.

If your proposal is worth writing, it is worth the support of all the sources that are sympathetic to your educational cause. The more local the funding source, particularly if it is a foundation or corporation, the more likely it is that a local friend of the school district can influence the decision. But you must ask them to help you.

Rule 6 — Ask for the specific amount of money you need to complete the project or for the portion of the full amount that the grantor is likely to fund, based on their granting history and pattern. Your research (homework) will tell you the funder's interests and level of support for education. If your project requires more funding than the grantor usually gives, identify the other funders you will be approaching and report any funds you have already been fortunate enough to acquire.

A proposal is not a shopping list. You should not give the funding source a choice of projects or a range of contributions. "Ask and ye shall receive" is a basic tenet of grantseeking. Give the funder a clear description of your project and specify the amount you expect from them. This will keep you from falling prey to the "Dear Occupant, Please Send Money" approach that often results in a check for $100 when you wanted $10,000.

Where do I begin? Most grantseekers are so focused on what *they* want to do and why *they* want to do it that they forget to take into consideration the reason(s) a funding source would be interested in supporting their projects, programs, and so on. This is the old "you can't see the forest for the trees" syndrome.

Many grantseekers begin the grants process by focusing on who has money. They then they try to develop a proposal that will appeal to the funding source, whether it be federal, state, foundation, or corporate. Frequently they are enticed into the grants process when they learn of the availability of grant funds through a colleague, a district publication, a professional journal, or a newsletter. Unfortunately, this sequence of events sets in motion a *reactive grants system* that is deadline driven. A reactive grants system often results in undue stress and tension, hastily prepared proposals, and usually rejection.

Do not fall into the trap of reactive grantseeking. Most funding sources have been making grants for years and function according to time frames that remain relatively consistent year after year. There are few surprises in the grants field, except for the number of grantees who do not learn from their fellow grantseekers' mistakes. Unless the funding source is newly established and has never published deadlines or made any awards, there is no excuse for not doing your homework and using public records to uncover as much information as possible about the funder.

To determine how to get started in grantseeking, you must first decide to be a proactive grantseeker. *Proactive grantseeking starts* with recognizing the needs of your students and then developing ideas, projects, and *solutions* to meet those needs. Armed with solutions, you *then* search for a source to fund them. When you develop a program, project, or idea that benefits your school/community and students and *then* seek out a funder, you establish two important convictions in the mind of a potential grantor.

First, your project/program is based upon your needs. The idea or solution has not been forced upon you by a funding source but rather is based upon your assessment of the need and your determination to develop a solution. In a proactive grants system you can provide a prospective funder with the minutes from the school/community or school advisory committee meetings at which the problem was discussed and innovative ways to solve it were brainstormed. Unfortunately, I have worked for school districts that attempted to make up minutes from such meetings to satisfy the funder's requests for a documented concern about a problem. Just remember that your school's credibility is at stake here.

When the funding source asks to see minutes, what they really want to be sure that:

- you identified the problem before they (the funding source) announced that they had money to deal with it, and that

- parents, teachers, and students were involved in developing solutions to the problem.

Second, you are approaching the prospective funder with a program that allows them to meet their needs at a price they can afford. Most prospective grantees become consumed by their projects and are unwilling to view the projects and their benefits from the funding source's point of view. By choosing a funding source because of their values, motives, and needs, you will develop a convincing proposal that demonstrates your knowledge of what the grantor funds, and why. In the process, you convince the funder that rather than being one of many you are approaching, they are the best possible partner in creating educational change for your students.

Funding sources do not want to feel that you are throwing proposals at every possible grantor. They want to know that you target your prospects and aim for the funder that would benefit the most from making a grant to your school.

The funding source wants to feel special. You *selected them* to work with you in producing the educational change. You were not reacting to their announcement of a deadline but to the match between your program's goals and their values and expectations.

In conclusion, a successful grants strategy is based on proactive grantseeking. If, for example, you have determined that your students could benefit educationally from computer-assisted technology, you would not:

- shotgun the same proposal to numerous funding sources,

- beg and plead with the potential grantor, and

- focus on your need for only one piece of equipment.

You would look at the need from the funding source's point of view. Funding sources are concerned about issues such as:

- how many students you will be able to influence over the usable life of the equipment,

- what the students will be able to do that they cannot do now,

- how your educational program will be adapted to integrate the use of their equipment,

- how the equipment and program will be demonstrated to other teachers,
- what, if any, parts of your program are innovative or different,
- whether you could present your program at a professional meeting, and
- whether you could publish or submit a description of the results of your program to an educational newsletter or journal.

The techniques presented in this primer will provide you with life-long grantseeking skills that you can use again and again. Whether you are seeking grants for preschool, after-school programs, or community and parent education, with the help of this book, you *will* find them.

CHAPTER TWO

Getting Ready to Seek Grants Support

Chapter 1 cautions against the "shotgun" approach to grantseeking. This chapter outlines a successful strategy for replacing the Ready-Fire-Aim approach with a Ready-Aim-Fire system.

As already mentioned, there are two different ways to approach proposal development — reactively and proactively.

1. **The Reactive Grantseeking System** — Reactive grantseekers wait for a grantseeking opportunity to present itself. Often they are made aware of opportunities through a peer, a journal or newsletter, a grants coordinator, or a curriculum specialist. They then attempt to develop an innovative, creative, well-organized approach to solving a problem while they are in a state of frenzied confusion. Whether you are creating a model project, a demonstration grant, or a research proposal, it is difficult to develop a successful approach while under the pressure caused by acting reactively rather than proactively.

2. **The Proactive Grantseeking System** — Proactive grantseekers begin with a need or problem they wish to solve through grant funding. They view *problems* as *opportunities* to interest a funder in working *with them* to implement solutions that will improve education.

Imagine that a funding source appeared in your classroom with a shoe box filled with money and said, "I am granting this money to your school and putting you in charge of spending it. First, however, I need to know what areas, or problems, the money will be used for." What would your response be? Take a few minutes to list the problems/opportunities you would present to our fictitious grantor.

This process is analogous to that of a friend telephoning you to let you know that he just won a million dollars in the lottery. He asks you to suggest some vacation spots that you think he might like and then informs you that he intends to take you with him. You would probably not start out by telling your friend where you would like to go. First, you would ask some general questions to help clarify what *he* would enjoy. For example, does he want to take a winter or summer vacation? Would he like to visit a tropical island or go on an African safari? In other words, you would try to assess the needs and expectations of your traveling companion. You would definitely not focus on your lifelong dream of visiting a particular destination if your friend has no interest in that spot.

Think of a grant as an agreement to travel with the grantor on a journey that benefits the funder as well as your classroom and students. Today's educational needs provide many opportunities to work with funding sources. In order to determine the projects you will pursue, outline your opportunities in advance.

Outlining opportunities does not entail writing down all solutions. Instead, begin by brainstorming, either by yourself or with a grants advisory committee (see chapter 3), a list of the problems/opportunities that you *may* want to deal with. This will get you going on your quest for grants. Remember, to get organized for grants success, you have to *get started!*

Review your list of problems/opportunities and select one, two, or three areas in which you would like to develop solutions. By generating a list of needs (problems, areas of interest, and so on) that you would like to impact, you will begin to develop a proactive system based on locating funding sources that are interested in the same problems you are and are therefore likely to invest in your solutions.

Create a three-ring binder (a Grants Workbook) for each need or problem area that you have identified and label the binders appropriately. Some problem areas (opportunities) will be difficult to place in one workbook because they encompass several areas of the curriculum. In this case you may want to develop one multidisciplinary book. How you do this is not as important as getting organized, selecting the problem, and getting started.

Your Grants Workbook will act as your filing cabinet. Use it to file:

- journal articles, studies, surveys, human interest stories, and newspaper clippings that document the problem,

- committee notes and names of other teachers and parents who are interested in collaborating on solutions to the problem,

- details of solutions to each problem,

- pertinent information on potential funding sources, including notes on your contact with them and ways to tailor your proposal to fit their needs and values, and

- letters of endorsement, consortium agreements, subcontracts, and so on.

I have found that the most effective grantseeking aids are usually simple and easy to implement. For instance, by organizing a Grants Workbook for each area you are interested in, you will save hours of time when you actually begin to write your proposals. In addition, a Grants Workbook makes a positive impression on grants advisory committee members, school staff, and especially *funding sources.*

Setting Goals

What do you expect from the grants process, and what are you willing to invest in grantseeking?

Set your sights on developing two proposals for the areas of need you have identified. Follow the system outlined in this primer and you are likely to have a 50 percent success rate. This prediction is based on the assumptions that you will not submit proposals to funding sources that do not value your area of interest or your solutions and that you will work proactively.

The following is a list of goals that will help you win grant funds.

1. Set your sights on developing a predetermined number of solutions to the problem.

2. Develop a Grants Workbook.

3. Organize a grants advisory committee or group.

4. Target a specific number of funding sources to research. Approach the potential funders by phone and/or personal visit.

5. Write a predetermined number of proposals as a result of your contact with the potential funding sources.

Two to four hours per week is a reasonable amount of time to invest in the grants process. Organizing your grants effort and setting goals may require you to employ some time-management techniques and do some rearranging of your daily/weekly schedule. A slight change in your routine may allow you to avail yourself, your school, and your students of the benefits that grantseeking can provide. Successful grantseeking begins with you!

CHAPTER THREE

Increasing Grants Success Through Volunteers

It has been said that nothing is more powerful than an idea whose time has come. To a grantor, nothing is more compelling than a proposal that involves the community. I have been employed in school districts as a health education coordinator and a community education coordinator, and in both of these positions I learned the positive value of involving the community in the grants process by initiating a grants advisory committee.

The Grants Advisory Group

In chapter 2 you were encouraged to initiate the grantseeking process in a proactive manner by selecting the problem(s) or area(s) you want to address. The next step is to invite targeted individuals to attend a meeting of your grants advisory committee. (You may want to call it a grants advisory *group* since the word *committee* sometimes strikes fear in people's hearts.)

You may choose to identify the grants group with one particular problem/opportunity. This will reduce confusion if you implement other grants advisory groups to attack other problem areas.

Before organizing a grants advisory group, I encourage you to check with your principal and/or coordinator for any district policies, concerns, and available assistance. Try to keep the group focused, manageable, and relaxed. (The word *group* connotes an informal relationship where one can come and go without a membership vote, and so on.)

One important result of a grants advisory group is community involvement and empowerment. But first, the group must *understand* the problem. The first meeting should be informative and aimed at setting goals for action. Use some of the information provided in chapter 6 to develop the group's knowledge about the grants marketplace. This information will enthuse them about developing solutions to the problem.

To get them started, encourage the group to react to any solutions that you may offer. Also encourage the members to brainstorm their own solutions and projects. The group needs to develop ownership and to "buy into" the needs and solutions. It is critical to your grants success to inform them of the effect that contacting funding sources has on the positive outcome of the grants process. Studies have demonstrated a 300 to 500 percent increase in the success rate of proposals when the funding sources are contacted informally *before* the proposals are written. This entails contact well in advance of any deadline.

Your group members need to know that they play an integral role in grantseeking. Although only one person writes the proposal (usually you), all group members play a vital role in the grants process. Their most important function is to share any links they have to potential funding sources. While their initial response is likely to be that they do not know anyone who could help in the process, a little digging will probably uncover contacts they didn't realize they had.

There are several techniques for bringing your group members to a level of commitment that assures that they will share their contacts and resources. Remember, the underlying reason for the volunteer to become involved in the first place is his or her desire to seek solutions, reduce a problem, and/or make educational advances for students all over the nation and in your school or classroom in particular.

The following worksheets and sample letters will help you organize your grantseeking effort and guide you in involving volunteers in the process. They include:

- Worksheet for Planning a Grants Advisory Group
- Grants Resources Inventory Worksheet

Instructions for Planning and Initiating a Grants Advisory Group

Once you have selected the area or need the group will focus on, you are ready to consider who could provide the assistance you need in developing preproposal contact and implementing a pro-active grants plan. Utilize the Worksheet for Planning a Grants Advisory Group (fig. 3.1) to help you.

Your choice of group members is very important. Do not put people on your grants advisory group solely because they are concerned and motivated. You need to have group members who can contact grant decision makers.

Your group sould be composed of a mix of the seven categories listed on the worksheet (parents, corporate leaders, foundation board members, college professors/educators, retired teachers, wealthy/influential people, and other). The best choices within each category depend on the skills and resources needed. One technique that works well is to invite a few key individuals to help you develop a list of potential group members.

Inventory of Linkages and Resources

One of the most fascinating aspects of your grants advisory group will be the wealth of resources you uncover that have never been utilized for education. Some grantseekers are aware that a local family-foundation board member on a committee may translate into a grant from that foundation, but few are aware of the resources that can be tapped in each volunteer's extended family of relatives, friends, and acquaintances.

You will be amazed to discover whom your advocates know — contacts you never thought you could touch. *Touch* is the correct word, even at the risk of sounding like a telephone company, since the billions granted by foundations and corporations are made *by* people *to* people. If the grantor knows you or knows about your program or classroom through a common linkage or friend, your proposal *will* get pushed to the top of the pile. One of the first lessons you will teach your grants advisory group is that just because a proposal is superbly written does not guarantee it will be funded. First it has to be read!

Don't get nervous. I am not suggesting that you abandon your teaching to become a grantseeking guru. I am just suggesting that the more volunteers you involve in the excitement of brainstorming solutions and projects, the more linkages they will share, and the more *work* they will do for your students.

It is critical to emphasize at this juncture that making preproposal contact with a funding source is the most important strategy that a grantseeker can employ.

When volunteers and advocates are armed with the proper information, they can play a

WORKSHEET FOR PLANNING
A GRANTS ADVISORY GROUP

Review the suggested categories of individuals to include and write down names.

Whom to Invite

________Parents

________Corporate Leaders

________Foundation Board Members

________College Professors/Educators

________Retired Teachers

________Wealthy/Influential People

________Others (Please Add)

Review the "Skills/Resources Needed" list below and write the underlined key resource description next to the possible committee members you have listed above. Avoid inviting volunteers who are overzealous about children but have no resources or contacts.

Skills/Resources Needed
- **Commitment** to children and education
- **Contacts** with people on foundation/corporate boards
- **Travel** to areas of the state/nation where there are more funders
- Willingness to share **telephone credit card** for grant-related calls
- **Marketing/sales skills**
- **Budgeting** and financial analysis skills
- Access to equipment and materials necessary to produce **audiovisual** aids depicting need
- Other

valuable role in making preproposal contact.

First, volunteers and advocates give your project even more credibility than you do. Yes, you are the initiator, the implementer, the expert, and the author of the proposal, *but* you also receive:

- the prestige accompanying a funded proposal,
- the money to spend, and
- the challenge of running the project.

Volunteers do not receive the same benefits. In fact, they often take time from their *own* children, jobs, and hobbies to work toward a greater good for *all* the students in your classroom and school.

Second, the more your advocates and volunteers take part in the grants process, the less work you will have to do. Your role will be that of a team leader who coordinates the work of others.

What you need is an inventory of the linkages and resources of your volunteers and advocates and a way of reminding them that their relatives, friends, and acquaintances can, or know people who can, get you an appointment with a funding official. Although there are vast differences in the accessibility of the various types of funders, a linkage makes a big difference in getting an appointment even when a paid bureaucrat is in charge of the grant program you are pursuing.

It is particularly difficult to get an appointment with a foundation official. This is because fewer than 1,000 of the existing 33,000 foundations have offices. In addition, there are only 3,000 foundation employees *in total.* Add to this the fact that most corporations prefer to have their employees volunteer at the nonprofit organizations they make grants to. In fact, some corporate grant applications ask potential grantees to list the company's employees who serve on the applicant's board. In the case of a grant for elementary or middle school education, the corporation may ask that you list their employees who volunteer at your school.

I suggest that you have at least one meeting with your grants advisory group to stimulate their interest in solving the problem and to foster trust and communication. Once that has been accomplished, make the group members aware of the facts about preproposal contact. After reading chapter 6, "Understanding the Grants Marketplace," and chapter 7, "Researching Potential Funders," you will be able to provide your grants advisory group members with a list of potential grantors and the names of their program personnel and board members. Ask your grant advisory group members to review the list and provide you with any links they have to the grantors. Encourage them to think of indirect as well as direct connections. Your group members may know someone who knows the grantor or belongs to the same organization.

Another valuable source of support your group members can provide to your grants quest are their personal resources. Distribute the Grants Resources Inventory Worksheet (fig. 3.2). Ask your group members to designate the types of assistance they would be willing to provide to your grants effort.

Bauer and Ferguson have developed a user-friendly software package that provides a way for you to organize and manage your linkages so that you always know who has the ability to get your foot in the door with a particular funding source. The program, *Winning Links,* operates on an IBM or IBM-compatible in either the 5.25" or 3.5" format. If you are interested in obtaining more information about this webbing and linkages software program, call 1-800-662-6642.

The more your volunteers understand the proactive grantseeking process, the more they will want to be involved in it. While the reactive approach makes grantseeking seem like a frenzied, chaotic, last-minute ordeal, proactive grantseeking is an exciting and productive mechanism for developing resources.

In an efficient grants system, the correct use of the skills, linkages, and brainpower of volunteers will reap benefits for your school time and time again. Volunteers do not want to address envelopes and lick stamps. They want to be a part of the funding equation. They want to be catalysts for *change!*

Figure 3.2

GRANTS RESOURCES INVENTORY WORKSHEET

Please put a check mark next to any resource area in which you can help. Use the section at the end of the worksheet to briefly describe the resources you could provide. If you are willing to contact funding sources, please list the areas of the United States that you visit frequently.

RESOURCE AREA

________ Evaluation of Projects

________ Computer Programming

________ Computer Equipment

________ Printing

________ Layout and Design Work

________ Budget Skills, Accounting, Developing Cash Flow, Auditing

________ Purchasing Assistance

________ Audiovisual Assistance (equipment, videotaping, etc.)

________ Travel

________ Long Distance Telephone Calls

________ Searching for Funding Sources

________ Sales Skills

________ Writing Skills/Editing Skills

________ Other Equipment/Materials

________ Other

Description of Resources: ____

Areas Frequently Visited: ____

CHAPTER FOUR

Developing a Motivating and Compelling Needs Statement

The first three chapters assured you that there are a lot of grant funds out there and volunteers to help you while cautioning you to avoid the major pitfalls of grantseeking (shotgunning the same proposal to several funders and last-minute reactive grantseeking). They also introduced you to the concept of viewing the needs of your school/community, classroom, and students from the funding source's point of view. *Remember the No/Know Rule — NO Funder Cares about What You Want; You must KNOW What the Funder Wants.* Funding sources are concerned about what *they* want and what *they* need. While it is true that each year government funding sources *must* expend all of their grant funds and that foundations *must* expend at least 5 percent of the value of their assets, these funding sources are not at a loss for potential grantees. In addition, corporate grantors can choose how many grants they make. They do not *have* to expend a portion of their profits. While many corporations choose to donate a percentage of their profits each year to nonprofit organizations, they, as well as government sources and foundations, have freedom of choice. They will award their support to the proposals that appear to promote the programs *they* value in the areas of need *they* care about. Therefore, it is imperative that you learn as much as you can about how a potential funding source views the need or the opportunity that your proposal will address.

Many grantseekers forget to ask themselves a critical question — WHO CARES?

- Who cares if the problem is reduced or solved?

- Who cares about our students and their education?

- Who cares if our curriculum is improved?

- Who cares if we promote new skills?

By asking the "who cares" questions early in the grantseeking process you will avoid frustration, rejection, and a lot of wasted time. Remember, you are going to approach a funder requesting support to help solve a problem you feel is so important that you have *already* dedicated your time and resources to developing solutions.

There are two excellent reasons why you should ask yourself and your grants advisory group who would care if you completed your project, bought your equipment, or continued or expanded your program. The first reason is that the answer will help you decide when it is time to abandon grantseeking as a plausible tool. The second reason is that the answers to the "who cares" questions will help you identify the funding sources that will be the most responsive to and interested in your project.

It is important that you know when to quit. The grants process may not provide you with the results you expect or desire. If only a few funders in your geographic area care about or value the outcome of your project, you may have to alter the project significantly or give it up. This advice may appear negative or defeatist, especially coming from an author and grantseeker known for his motivational speeches, persistence, and positive attitude. It is true that I rarely give up. But if there aren't enough potential funding sources that are concerned about the need for your project, you may have to change or abandon it. Unfortunately, you believe that the problem is so pressing that you *have to* do it. This is where some grantseekers go astray. Many grantseekers are so emotionally involved in their projects that they move directly to the solution. If you start with the solution instead of the need, you become narrow in your focus and concentrate on what *you want to do* instead of the need and who cares about it.

Grantseekers with a narrow focus and a great deal of conviction (some are actually almost possessed) believe that they could get their project funded if they could get to the funder in person and convince them to value the change the project will bring about. Listen to the advice of someone who has spent a lifetime trying to instill health-related values in children and adults. Your zeal, persistence, and other positive personal characteristics cannot change another person's values. The fact is that most private funders (foundations and corporations) do not even read proposals that do not interest or appeal to them.

So what *can* you do to increase your grants success? The successful grants system is composed of the following five steps.

1. Develop and document the need or problem (opportunity).
2. Propose several solutions.
3. Identify, through research, possible grantors that may be responsive to and interested in your project.
4. Contact the grantor (directly or through a linkage) to gather information that will help you choose the solution that will be the most appealing to the potential funding source.
5. Write the proposal.

Following these five steps *in order* is critical to your success. Many grantseekers believe that the project they want to get funded is so important, interesting, and creative that they skip the first four steps and *begin* by writing their proposal. Then they practice reactive grantseeking or spend a few minutes searching on a computer for funders before setting out to hunt grants with their shotguns.

The basics for gathering data on the need for any project or solution are founded on the principle that individuals see and hear what *they* want in a proposal. To help you understand this process, I have developed the Values Approach to Grantseeking. Each of us, including grantors, develops a set of values that guides us through our lives. This internal guidance system is based upon a variety of influences, including culture, religion, family, friends, education, and so on.

The values we develop define our reality and, once formed, provide the basis for what we believe to be true (not what *is* true, but what we *believe* to be true). When we are presented with facts, proposals, and situations, we attend to what is consistent with our beliefs.

Think of these values as a pair of prescription glasses. Each of us has developed a distinct and different pair, and therefore we all view the world differently. These prescription glasses have a pair of prescription hearing aids attached to them. The lenses and the hearing aids act as filters to help us attend to and store information that matches our prescription and reinforces what we believe. In essence, we each hear and see what we want to! Conversely, we ignore what we don't value. Complementing this theory is my conviction that we are all entitled to our own prescription glasses (or values) as long as we operate within our society's laws.

I know of few things that demonstrate an individual's values more than how they spend their money. Grantors can be divided into three groups (government, foundation, and corporate). Each of these types of funding sources and their values glasses will be discussed in chapter 6. At this point, it is only important that you realize that you must be knowledgeable about grantors' values or you run the risk of assuming that they use the same prescription lenses as you to view the world. In fact, I believe that the main problem with 50 percent of rejected proposals is that the prospective grantee assumes that the funding source's values are the same as his or hers.

The first step to grants success is to develop and document the need or problem (opportunity). Never *start* with a solution unless you are independently wealthy and can fund your own project! If you have not chosen your parents carefully or won the lottery, begin by gathering many types of data to document the *need* for your project. You must gather several types of data because at this stage you do not know:

- whom you will approach;
- what they will value in your problem and solution, or
- what will make them *best* "see" the need and hence feel a compelling motivation to fund it.

This Values Approach to Grantseeking will help you know what to present and how to present it to each particular grantor as well as what not to say to avoid a values conflict. Even when you and the grantor have many values in common, presenting the need for your project in the wrong way may repel a funding source. Funding sources make grants for their reasons, not yours.

It is imperative that you learn the Golden Rule of Grantseeking: *He or She Who Has the Gold Makes the Rules and the Grants!*

Documenting the Need

The needs section of a proposal has several different names, including:

- Needs Statement,
- Search of Relevant Literature,
- Statement of the Problem, and
- Areas to Be Addressed.

No matter what it is called, its purpose is the same — to provide the grantor with:

- *Substantiating evidence* that the writer has a command of the current state of the art in his or her field and knows what is going on in his or her classroom and school and in other schools.
- *Statistics, surveys,* and other *data* that document the extent of the problem in the writer's school. This includes, but is not limited to, such items as standardized test scores to develop a clear picture of the extent of the problem.

- *Case Studies* that give human interest to needs documentation. Studies and statistics tend to be viewed merely as numbers. While they are factual, they may not convey to the reader that the proposal is really about students, children, future leaders, and workers in our society. A quotation or an example of what it is like to be part of the needs population can be very moving to some funders. Although these examples need to be real, the names should be changed to protect individuals' identities. *Note:* Do not take all of your examples and condense them into one fictitious person. Use real cases only. For example, "Melissa's story is typical in my classroom. . . ."

- *Quotations* from authorities in the field whose opinions may be viewed positively by a potential funder. Authorities might include local and/or national experts, elected officials, police, individuals who work with children, and so on.

Once you have selected and prioritized the areas you want to address, begin searching for needs documentation in your classroom, school, school system, and publications. (Note that you may have to remove your prescription values glasses to collect the variety of data necessary to document the need to someone who views the world differently from you.) Store your needs data in the appropriate section of your Grants Workbook (see chapter 2). When you know whom you will approach with a proposal and what they value, you will role play looking at the need through their values glasses in order to select the most compelling and motivating descriptions of the need. What you will ultimately do is present a case that convinces the funder that a grant must be made *now* to reduce the problem you have presented by means of the solution you are recommending.

Remember that the need is the difference or gap between what is now and what should be. Each day that the needs gap is not addressed, the problem grows. Closing this gap reduces the problem and is the reason for the funding source to read the needs section of your proposal and ultimately to fund your solution.

Figure 4.1

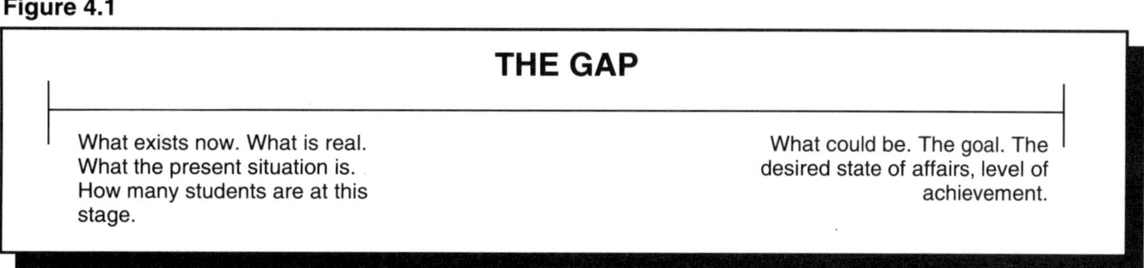

Complete the Needs and Goals Worksheets (figs. 4.2 and 4.4). Included are several examples of completed worksheets to guide you in developing a motivating and compelling case for your project.

Your time is valuable, and you must use it wisely to employ successful grantseeking techniques. My Values Approach to Grantseeking will pay dividends in success rates and dollars, considering the small investment of time you make now to describe the need. In addition, it will help you believe that you are presenting a grantor with an opportunity to take part in a project that will meet their needs at the same time that it meets education's needs and yours.

When you employ the more common approach to grantseeking (write proposal, look for any funder, send proposal), you do not get the confidence and the self-assurance that come from knowing you *started* from the *need* and then determined who would value the changes you are proposing. Making preproposal contact (chapter 8) is not difficult when your research already indicates that the potential funder is interested in and values what you want to do. You have the confidence that comes from doing your homework. Efficient grantseeking requires the same effort we require of our students. Students facing an exam feel confident if they have prepared for it. Your degree of comfort with your proposal is in proportion to the effort that went into preparing it.

Passing the exam is not the goal of education, and likewise, getting the cash is not the goal of grantseeking. The end you desire is the successful completion of the project and the funding source's respect.

The funding relationship is built on *trust,* and that trust starts with understanding how the funder views the need and the proposed solutions. This concern for the funder's need does not mean that you involve them in your classroom and abrogate your responsibilities as the educational decision maker. What it does mean is that you inspire their respect as an educator and leader in your field. The follow-up, the reporting, and the rapport you develop will result in a continuing relationship — not necessarily continuous grants, but continued interest and possibly more investment when another one of your projects meets that funder's needs.

UTILIZING THE NEEDS WORKSHEET AND THE GOALS WORKSHEET

Your completed worksheets will provide a clear picture of what is and what ought to be. The worksheets do not suggest ways to eliminate, close, or reduce the gap. Instead, they clarify:

- why the gap between what is and what ought to be must be closed
  or reduced, and
- what perspective on the need a funder must have to be interested
  in *any* solution.

These questions deal with the need as *you have* documented it. Many zealous grantseekers overlook the perspective of a funding source that has several, and often conflicting, interests. In such cases slight changes in your documentation can make the need appeal to funding sources with varying geographic interests. For instance:

- Can your need be documented for a funder that has an interest
  only in your classroom/school/community?
- Can you document the need on a county- or statewide basis?
- What is the national need to address this problem?
- Does the need exist internationally?

If you ask these questions while developing the need, you will be ready for the possible international grantor that has a facility in your community and another in Munich. Corporate funding officials may be interested in funding a project that develops math and science skills using the same conceptual solution in two different elementary schools in two different sites — your community and Munich. Naturally, the solution you develop to reduce the problem must correlate with the need you document.

Remember to view the need from various geographical perspectives—local, regional, state, national and international.

COMPLETING THE NEEDS WORKSHEET

State the problem or area that your grantseeking is intended to address. Write the data that document that the problem exists in the column titled "What Exists Now — The Present State of Affairs." Record the source of the data, including the date, on the right side of the worksheet in the column titled "Source of Data." A completed sample worksheet has been provided for your review. In the sample, the solutions deal with strategies to involve parents in their children's formal education and to make them aware of the influences that compete for a child's attention (e.g., television).

Even though everyone in your grants advisory group may agree that the problem area you described on the Needs Worksheet is indeed a problem, it *must* be backed up by evidence, not opinion. You can include the opinion of an expert as one form of documentation (e.g., the opinion of the president of the Parent- Teacher Association), but an opinion will help only when it substantiates the *facts*.

Most grantseekers list the problem indicators first when they begin to document the need. It is important to start with the indicators because they help individuals motivate themselves to make a difference and do something about the problem.

Complete the Needs Worksheet, but try to hold yourself and your volunteers back from moving quickly to solutions. You may find it helpful to have your grants advisory group review your completed worksheet and provide comments, additions, and so on. However, the best course of action would be to have a volunteer review the facts, conduct a search of the literature, and add

Figure 4.2

NEEDS WORKSHEET

Completing this worksheet will help you step back from possible solutions and projects and establish that there is a gap between what is now and what should be.

Problem Area: ____

____

____

Documentation of the Need to Address This Problem:

What Exists Now —   **Source of Data**
The Present State of Affairs
(Studies, Facts, Surveys,   (Organization)
  Case Studies, etc.)   (Journal, Newsletter, Newspaper, etc.)
                                      (Date of Publication)

Note: *Consider performing a survey of your classroom, school, and/or community to document that the problem exists.*

Figure 4.3

NEEDS WORKSHEET
SAMPLE

Completing this worksheet will help you step back from possible solutions and projects and establish that there is a gap between what is now and what should be.

Problem Area: Parents' lack of involvement in their children's formal education and lack of support for constructive informal educational experiences.

Documentation of the Need to Address This Problem:

What Exists Now —
The Present State of Affairs

Source of Data

4 out of 5 parents reported that they regularly discuss schoolwork with their children. Yet two-thirds of the children said their parents rarely or never talked about school with them.

Department of Education, Office of Educational Research and Improvement, Study reported in the *Wall Street Journal* on January 3, 1992. 25,000 middle school children surveyed.

Two-thirds of the parents claimed to place limits on television viewing. Two-thirds of the children said they had no limits on television viewing.

The middle school group (8th graders) reported watching 21.4 hours of television per week, in comparison to spending 5.6 hours per week on homework.

50% of the parents reported attending school meetings, but less than one-third had ever visited their child's classroom. 66% had never talked to school officials concerning their child's homework.

Note: *You could include findings from surveys of your classroom, school, or community; a consortium of classes; or a comparison to a classroom in Europe or another part of the world.*

---

to your base of knowledge. Remember, you will probably never use all the data you collect in *one* proposal, but the more data you have, the easier it will be to tailor your proposal to the particular perspective of a grantor.

COMPLETING THE GOALS WORKSHEET

Describe the problem area in the space provided. You may find it helpful to provide copies of the Needs Worksheet to those completing the Goals Worksheet so that they can address the question already posed on that worksheet.

When completing the Goals Worksheet, start by asking yourself what the situation would be like if the problem were solved. What would the students, school, classroom, district, parents, society be like? You are describing an ideal state of affairs. Naturally, not *all* children will reach their potential. We will not be able to *totally* eliminate prejudice or bigotry. But goals provide direction. They tell us where to aim. They are not usually measurable.

To help you legitimize and clarify your goal, use the space provided on the Goals Worksheet to list studies, quotations, and research findings that show that the direction you want to move in is justified and proper.

A completed sample worksheet has been provided for your review. In the sample, the problem described is parents' lack of involvement in their children's education. This problem has yielded a goal statement that answers the question "What if the problem were solved?" In this ideal state of affairs, parents and teachers would act as responsible partners and work together to maximize the educational achievement of children.

The next step will be to brainstorm strategies (solutions) for closing the gap you have documented.

GOALS WORKSHEET
SAMPLE

Problem Area: Parents' lack of involvement in their children's formal education and lack of support for constructive informal educational experiences.

If the needs documented on the Needs Worksheet were fulfilled and the problem was eliminated, what would result? What is the *desired* state of affairs? The ultimate end? The answer to these questions states the goal. The Needs Worksheet documents what exists now. The Goals Worksheet documents what ought to be. The goal provides purpose, direction, and motivation for grantseeking.

Goal: Parents and teachers acting as responsible partners who work together to maximize children's educational achievement.

Record studies, quotations, and research findings that document what ought to be. Provide sources and dates.

Studies — Quotations — Research Findings	Source — Date
Students whose parents discussed their schoolwork recorded higher grades.	Dept. of Education Study *Wall Street Journal* 1/3/92
Television viewing restrictions tended to boost grades.	Dept. of Education Study *Wall Street Journal* 1/3/92
"Burden of education should not be on the teachers and schools alone." Education Department study says, "Parents have a major role to play."	Dept. of Education Study *Wall Street Journal* 1/3/92
Home-based guidance program in Rochester schools demonstrates educational improvement in low income students. Homeroom teacher acts as liaison between schools and parents. When teacher makes home visits, children do better in school.	Harvard University, 3-year study, *Democrat & Chronicle* November 28, 1991.
Preschool children from single-parent homes have better verbal skills than children from two-parent homes (more one-on-one communication).	Unpublished study 1989-90 Deirdre Madden, Baldwin Wallace College, Berea, OH, *Democrat & Chronicle* November 28, 1991.
Harrison, Arkansas — Students score in top 10% of the nation in test scores, yet Arkansas ranks 272 of 327 in education taxes. One of the lowest tax rates in the U.S. Money may not be the resource that makes the difference. Parents volunteer in their children's classrooms one hour per week. Duties include: making copies, grading papers, working with students, listening to students read. Basically, the parents save teachers time. Parents and teachers meet on school councils and determine the educational goals for next year. Each school reports progress toward goals in a newspaper advertisement. School system received 10 new computers donated by civic clubs. Parents made speeches at clubs. Frank Newman, President of Education Commission, states, "They're saying parents are important and teachers are important and they should be part of running the schools."	*USA Today* 11/18/91 Study identifies good schools through "School Match" of Columbus, Ohio. "School Match" provides information to families moving to new areas.

Note: *This is not the place to list solutions. The means of closing the gap between what is now and what ought to be is the solution. The solution reduces the problem. It is discussed in Chapter 5.*

CHAPTER FIVE

Developing Solutions to Problems

Your task now is to increase your success in attracting grant funds to reduce or solve the problem you documented in chapter 4. At this point, many grantseekers believe that they're ready to write their proposals. They think that they have already identified the best possible solution, and they may have a deadline looming in the not-too-distant future.

But wait, have you considered alternative solutions? To avoid the narrow, self-centered focus of many grantseekers (typified by "I want to do this project my way"), keep in mind the Values Approach to Grantseeking, which focuses on the grantor's values.

You want to convince the grantor that you are an outcome-oriented grantseeker. It is critical that the solution you suggest will make a meaningful contribution to reducing the need and closing the gap between what is and what ought to be. In fact, you should generate *several* possible solutions to alleviating the problem.

Most grantseekers have only one solution (their favorite), and they *want to do it now!* Approaching the potential granting source with only one solution is risky. First, you may be perceived as narrow-minded. Funding sources prefer to think that you have considered many alternatives and chosen the best one. They may even want to know *why* you selected the chosen alternative over other options. Second, the solution you choose may not meet the granting source's expectations. For example, they may find your problem compelling but your solution very weak. Just as you might turn off a grantor with a needs statement that is not compatible with their values, you might propose the solution that is your choice only to discover that it is not the grantor's choice.

The fact that a proposal gets funded does not necessarily mean that it was well conceived, well written, or outstanding. It could be that the proposal simply presented the best solution in a specific area of the funding source's interest.

How do you develop and present the "best" solution to a grantor? One of the most vital steps in my Values Approach to Grantseeking is to generate alternative solutions to the problem. A well-conceived and well-thought-out solution is the bottom line in proposal generation.

What works best is to generate several potential solutions without spending a lot of time and energy on detail. The object is to make preproposal contact with the potential grantor and to try to involve them in choosing which solution to present in your proposal.

In your final grant proposal you must present *one* solution that will both impact the problem and be viewed positively by the funder. Your research on the prospective funding source will hopefully yield information that will help you choose that solution. Remember, you cannot present a "shopping list" of possible solutions or ideas in your final proposal. But the greater the number of good ideas you develop for approaching the problem, the better your chance of selecting the best solution.

Developing Your Knowledge of Previously Funded Proposals

Through your search of the literature and grantor research, you will be able to identify the schools and educational groups that have previously received funding in your problem area and what solutions they proposed. Developing your knowledge concerning the success and failure of past grants will help you

- know which approaches to discuss with prospective grantors,
- avoid duplicating a failed proposal,
- suggest new approaches that capitalize on the experiences of past grantees, and
- inform members of your grants advisory group of what solutions have been proposed and thereby provide a basis for generating new ideas.

1. Who Should Help You Develop and Improve Your Proposal Ideas. Grantors are leery of grantseekers whose solutions do not take into account the opinions of others. Grant makers are much more sophisticated than we may want to acknowledge. They know that the "best" approach takes into consideration the concerns, criticisms, and improvements of many individuals. Even in cases where grant makers do not allow any preproposal contact, they want you to consider the opinions of other experts in developing your approach. While you may still say "I" in your proposal, the sense you want to convey to the prospective grantor is that several individuals, groups, and/or organizations have been involved in generating, critiquing, and endorsing the chosen solution.

The following is a list of potential partners for developing and improving your proposal ideas

- your grants advisory group
- fellow educators from your school and other schools
- administrators in your school — including curriculum specialists, school coordinators, and so on
- students — current elementary and middle school students, high school students, graduates of your system, dropouts (indicating that the current system failed)
- parents
- concerned community members
- college/university professors and other professionals in the field of education
- political allies and elected officials or their administrative assistants

2. How to Generate Ideas. Years of experience have shown me that you do not need to hold a formal meeting of your key partners in order to develop and improve your proposal ideas. Other than during a scheduled meeting of your grants advisory group, it is best to approach your other partners in small, informal groups or individually. The most creative solutions are often arrived at over a cup of coffee or on a work break.

Nor do you need to set aside large blocks of undisturbed time to create unique solutions. In fact, most experts say that a time restriction of five to eight minutes should be observed when groups are brainstorming solutions. The following guidelines have worked for me with my grants advisory committees and small groups of selected individuals.

- Give the participants a brief description of the problem you are trying to solve. You may even decide to distribute your Needs and Goals Worksheets to establish the gap that the solution will seek to reduce.
- Tell your participants that their goal is to generate ideas about and solutions to the stated problem.
- Set a five-minute time limit for expressing ideas.
- Appoint an individual to record the suggestions.

(Note: In some cases, I include information on what solutions have already been attempted.)

How to Use the Worksheet for Developing Solutions and Projects to Reduce the Problem

List the group's proposed solutions on the Worksheet for Developing Solutions and Projects to Reduce the Problem (fig. 5.1). Make a copy of the completed worksheet for each participant and ask each to rank order the solutions, with number 1 indicating her or his favorite. This will help you analyze and evaluate the ideas.

How to Use the Worksheet for Developing the Top Five Suggested Solutions to the Problem

Ask the group to focus on their five favorite solutions. Jot them down on the Worksheet for Developing the Top Five Suggested Solutions to the Problem (fig. 5.2). Discuss and record the advantages and disadvantages of each of the five solutions.

Ask the group to arrive at a rough cost estimate of each of the solutions. However, at this point, do not eliminate an approach because it seems expensive. Since you do not have any money yet, why place cost constraints on your ideas? Encourage your participants to explore solutions that cost different amounts of money.

A completed sample worksheet has been included for your review (fig. 5.3). In the example, the group rank ordered all proposed solutions on a Worksheet for Developing Solutions and Projects to Reduce the Problem. They then transferred the top five solutions to the Worksheet for Developing the Top Five Suggested Solutions to the Problem. It is important to note that the five listed solutions are not mutually exclusive and that the integration of several strategies can sometimes yield an exemplary proposal for a model project.

In this example, the educator and parents advisory group decided that the most interesting combination was to involve students, parents, and teachers in developing a learning contract for each month. They decided to report to parents on student progress by means of videotapes and home and school visits.

In your situation, the process will encourage your volunteers to "buy into" the solution and result in their continued support of the rest of the grants process.

WORKSHEET FOR DEVELOPING SOLUTIONS AND PROJECTS TO REDUCE THE PROBLEM

Problem: ____

____

____

____

List any and all proposed solutions. No discussions, please. Discuss the ideas after the time allotted for brainstorming has expired. Then request each participant to rank order the proposed solutions, with 1 being the favorite.

Rank   **Proposed Solutions/Projects to Reduce the Problem**

-
-
-
-
-
-
-
-
-
-
-
-
-
-
-
-
-

WORKSHEET FOR DEVELOPING THE TOP FIVE SUGGESTED SOLUTIONS TO THE PROBLEM

Problem: ____

____

Describe the top five proposed solutions briefly and give a rough estimate of the cost of each. Also provide an estimate of the cost per student or teacher. Include the number of individuals who would benefit directly from each solution and the number who could benefit indirectly through duplication of the approach at other schools. List the drawbacks of each (i.e., those things that would impede its success).

Ask the following of each solution. Would you fund this idea with a grant? Will the benefits justify the money expended?

Solution #1:

Solution #2:

Solution #3:

Solution #4:

Solution #5:

WORKSHEET FOR DEVELOPING THE TOP FIVE SUGGESTED SOLUTIONS TO THE PROBLEM
SAMPLE

Problem: Parents' lack of involvement in their children's formal elementary and middle school education and lack of support for constructive informal educational experience.

Describe the top five proposed solutions briefly and give a rough estimate of the cost of each. Also provide an estimate of the cost per student or teacher. Include the number of individuals who would benefit directly from each solution and the number who could benefit indirectly through duplication of the approach at other schools. List the drawbacks of each (i.e., those things that would impede its success).

Ask the following of each solution. Would you fund this idea with a grant? Will the benefits justify the money expended?

Solution #1: Develop a parent-teacher-student education contract that outlines each party's responsibility to support education. Review and renew every month on a three-part carbonless form.

Solution #2: Send home to the parents a short videotape of classroom and educational techniques and add a specific segment on the parents' child and her or his progress.

Solution #3: Require teachers to visit every student's home twice per year to report on the child's educational progress.

Solution #4: Allow taxpayers to lower their school taxes by volunteering/working at the school.

Solution #5: Send parents a newsletter each month with articles on how and why they should get involved.

CHAPTER SIX

Understanding the Grants Marketplace

If you have a specific grantor's program announcement and only one or two weeks to prepare your proposal, you do not have time to read this chapter. This chapter is intended for proactive grantseekers who are looking for the best match between their proposal ideas and a grantor's needs. Reactive grantseekers whose rejected proposals prove they did not locate the "right" funder in their latest attempts at grantseeking will also find this chapter worthwhile, especially if they decide to incorporate preproposal contact into their future grantseeking attempts.

Just as teachers face a myriad of questions from well-intentioned seekers of knowledge (their students), I am asked questions by my well-intentioned students — grantseekers searching for the secret to grant funding. The two most common questions I am asked are:

- Where should I go for grant funding? (Which grants marketplace will provide me with the best opportunity? Corporations? Foundations? Government?)

- Once I know the marketplace, how do I find the best grantor for my project?

The obvious solution is for me to tell them the correct answers. But, as a teacher, I am not supposed to give the answers. I am supposed to help my students find them. Teachers want students to develop the concepts that will organize the students' data and lead them to discover the answers for themselves. We all know how much more difficult it is to teach the process than to give the answers.

Recently a participant at one of my grants seminar asked me to explain how I select a type of funding source and a specific grantor for a project idea. As I analyzed the process I use, I was reminded of my high school geometry teacher. (After several years in her class we came to know each other quite well.) My geometry teacher would present a problem and the postulates to use in proving the theorem. In a frenzy of confusion and with time running out, I often pleaded that I just did not know *where to start*. Her response was, "Well, it is obvious where to begin. Take postulate number three and . . ." But what was obvious to the specialist, my geometry teacher, was not obvious to me, the geometry student. The teacher knew the answer, the geometric concepts, and the correct approach. My approach was to try each postulate until something worked. (Unfortunately, the problem then became a permutation-combination and took ten hours to solve.) I never did pass the course, but while my failure did not have a drastic effect on my career, you and your projects are critically important.

Your problem is to determine where to get the money for your project. To figure this out, you need to develop your knowledge of the general types of funding sources and their major differences and similarities. The Grantseekers' Decision Matrix will help you develop the insights you need to find the funder best suited to your school and your project.

Use the matrix each time you begin the process of selecting the most appropriate grantor for your project. This system follows the Values Approach to Grantseeking developed in the previous chapters and is based upon how the funder views the need for the project and your qualifications. Using the matrix will give you a rough assessment of the potential interest of the various types of funders. Grantors are not easy to characterize, and there are many generalizations represented on the matrixes. However, it would not be helpful to *begin* by looking at grantors that do not fit the general rule. Nor would it be helpful to begin by overwhelming you with information on each individual granting source. The purpose of the matrix is to provide you with a logical place to start your search for the "best" funder.

Grantseekers' Decision Matrix

The matrix has the following ten columns: Type of Funder, Geographic Need, Type of Project, Award Size, School's Image, Credentials of Project Director, Preproposal Contact, Proposal Content, Review System, and Grants Administration. The following is a description of each funder type. Chapter 7 provides details on how to move from the type of funder to their individual granting programs.

COLUMN 1 — TYPE OF FUNDER.

This column lists nine major funding sources. Together they award approximately $100 billion each year in grants.

1. Federal—The federal government provides over $75 billion in grants through 1,225 separate granting programs.

To understand government grant support for elementary and middle schools, you must remember that our country's founders decreed that responsibility for any functions not specified in the Constitution rests with state and local governments. The United States Department of Education is not responsible for educating our children. We, at the local level, are responsible.

The federal role has traditionally been to supply grant monies to initiate and, in some cases, support educational programs that affect many or all of the states. Federal programs that support the educational concerns of *one* area of the United States are funded by revenue from taxes paid by citizens *across* the United States.

The Elementary and Secondary Schools Act empowers federal involvement in state and local schools. (The Department of Education defines who is eligible to receive their funds. Eligible organizations are called Local Educational Agencies or LEAs.) Programs funded by the Elementary and Secondary Schools Act are referred to as title or chapter grants. You should always check with your district superintendent's office to see if your project or idea might be covered by a title grant. Some entitlement programs have funds for special projects. In addition, the federal contact person may advise you of other programs appropriate for your projects and ideas.

The Department of Education believes it can improve education by sponsoring grant competitions that encourage educational research and innovative approaches to education. While the federal government does support continuing programs like Head Start and Early Start, the Department's basic role is to initiate, prove, and/or demonstrate. The continuation or implementation of a proven model is the responsibility of the state and local school district.

GRANTSEEKERS' DECISION MATRIX

Type Funder	Geographic/Need	Type of Project	Grant Award Size For Field on Int	School's Image	Credentials of P.I. or P.D.	Preproposal Contact •Any Face-to-Face is +	Proposal Content	Review System	Grants Administration (Rules)
1. Federal	Varies–but must have national/international	Model Innovation Research	Large	Very national image+	National Image	Write, phone, go and see	Extensive–many forms long	Staff and peer review. Human subjects & animals	Many/compiles OM B cir audits + match $
2. State	State/Local Need	Model and Replication	Medium Small	Statewide image+	Statewide image	Write, phone, go and see	Extensive–many forms long	Staff and some peer review	Many/complex audits + match $
3. National General-Purpose	National Need–Local ,Regional Population	Model Innovative	Large Medium	National image+	National +	Write, phone	Short–concept paper then longer longer if interested	Staff and some peer review	Few audits and rules
4. Special Purpose	Need in area of interest	Model Innovative Research	Large to Small	Image not as critical as solution is	Image in field of interest+	Write, phone	Short–concept paper– longer form if interested	Board review (some staff)	Few audits and rules
5. Community	Local Need	Operation Replication Building Equipment	Small	Local image+	Respected locally	Write, phone, go and see	Short–letter proposal	Board review	Few audits and rules
6. Family	Varies–but geographic concern for need	Innovation Replication Building/Equipment some research	Medium Small	Regional image+	Local/regional	Write, phone	Short–letter proposal	Board	Very few audits and rules
7. Corporate–Large	Near plants or offices	Product Development Replication Building Equipment	Medium Small	Local image + Employee involvement	Local, national	Write, phone, go and see	Short–letter proposal	Contributions Committee	Very few audits and rules
8. Corporate–Small	Very near to company	Same	Medium Small	Local image critical	Local	Write, phone, go and see	Short–letter proposal	Owner/Family	Very few audits and rules
9. Nonprofit Organizations and Service Clubs	Local	Replication Building Equipment. Scholarship.	Small	Local image and member involvement	Local	Write, phone, present to committee or to members	Short–letter proposal	Committee review and/or member vote	Few rules and audit

Therefore, the federal government is *not* a good source to approach for continuing or reinstating a program that your district will no longer support. You will have much better results if you turn to federal funding sources for support for programs that develop innovative or creative models for change in education.

With a budget of over $30 billion for DOE, the federal government should be your first choice when you are looking for support for new programs.

2. State—State grants programs are established and supported through state tax dollars. The amount of state grant funds available varies greatly, and the projects these funds support depend on each state's educational programs and unique needs.

States also make grants with funds received from the federal government. These funds are designated by law to pass through the state. There are many education funds your state receives as a result of a formula or criteria related to needs, population, and so on. The state may pass on the money as a grant to all eligible schools or may use competition through proposals as a means of disseminating these federal funds.

3. National General-Purpose Foundations—These are the large, well-known foundations. While they number fewer than 100 of the total 34,000 foundations, they have hundreds of millions of dollars in assets. Of the $7 billion in grants awarded each year by foundations, they are the largest contributor.

National general-purpose foundations usually employ staff and may use experts in the field to review proposals. Most of the 3,000 individuals employed by foundations work for this group. National general-purpose foundations fund a wide variety of interests and do so on the national and local levels, and in some instances, internationally. They often have an interest in educational innovation and education as it relates to minorities and economic concerns. They spend a good deal of time reading proposals, meet more often than smaller foundations, and are often available for preproposal contact. Examples in this group include the Ford Foundation and the Rockefeller Foundation.

4. Special-Purpose Foundations—These foundations support a relatively narrow range of grant interests. Numbering only a few hundred, they still constitute a major influence in their fields of choice. They have directors and staff and, similar to the large national general-purpose foundations, meet more often and spend more time reading proposals than other types of foundations.

5. Community Foundations—This is the fastest-growing type of foundation in respect to number and assets. These foundations are named after the geographic area they serve. There are currently over 300 community foundations. Some have full or part-time staff ,and the composition of their boards normally reflects the community they seek to enhance. Their funds are usually generated from bequests, and their grants must benefit the community they are located in. Examples include the Cleveland Foundation, the Chicago Foundation, and the San Diego Foundation.

6. Family Foundations—Family foundations account for approximately 80 percent of all foundations. However, they award less than 20 percent of all foundation grants. Only the largest of the 30,000 plus family foundations have a director, and few have staff. In fact, of the 34,000 total foundations, fewer than 1,000 have an office.

Family foundations normally award smaller grants and have little staff or peer review.

Their boards usually meet only one or two times a year for an average length of three hours. Therefore, decisions are made fast and without much opportunity for discussion with prospective grantees, either before or after the deadline.

To help you understand this marketplace, consider the following. There were only 57,443 grants for more than $10,000 in 1992. These grants totaled over $3.5 billion, or one-half of the $7 billion in total foundation grants. The other $3 billion plus was made up of hundred of thousands of grants for less than $10,000, and most of these came from family foundations. These grants went to approximately 500,000 tax-exempt groups. Only a small portion went to education, and only a part of those went to the estimated 71,887 elementary and middle schools in the United States.

7. Corporate—Large—Corporate (large) grants come from corporate funds and corporate foundation assets. There are over 2.3 million corporations in the United States and only a few thousand utilize a corporate foundation to make their grants. Some corporations make grants from both the corporation and the corporate foundation. The main difference between the two granting vehicles is that the corporate foundation allows for a more even distribution of grants because assets can be tapped to fund a more consistent granting program when profits are low. Another big difference is that only the corporate foundation's tax return is available for public scrutiny. Therefore, controversial grants are often made through the corporation without the knowledge of the public or the corporation's stockholders.

Corporate grants totaled over $6 billion in 1992 and have not kept pace with inflation for two consecutive years. A recent study showed that only 35 percent of corporations make contributions to nonprofit organizations. But, of those that do, education is a primary area of interest. Corporations are interested in how the grants they fund will affect their workers, the children of their workers, their profits, and their products.

A grant to your classroom offers them a chance to position their products with students, teachers, and parents and provides them with an opportunity to learn how to improve their products. These large corporations normally have a contributions officer in charge of their giving programs and spend more time reading proposals than some of the foundations. Having a corporation's employees volunteer at your school is critical to securing the corporation's support. Examples in the large corporate category include I.B.M., Apple Computer, 3M, Texaco, and Kodak.

8. Corporate—Small—It is difficult to find accurate information on the grantors in this category. While the data is scarce, these smaller corporations provide an excellent funding prospect for schools because they give where they live. In addition, these smaller corporations often have more ties to the community and its schools than other types of funding sources. The key to grants support from this group is their involvement in your school and its projects. Examples include small businesses, family businesses, and owner-operated franchises such as McDonald's, Jiffy Lube, Taco Bell, and so on.

9. Nonprofit Organizations and Service Clubs—This group includes professional associations, hellenic groups, business groups, service clubs, and membership groups. Many have an education or youth subcommittee that actively seeks projects worthy of their support. A list of service clubs is usually posted on a sign as you enter a community, and the sign often lists meeting places and times. Nonprofit organizations and service clubs can be approached to support parts of a costly proposal or a matching component, or to challenge other organizations to raise an amount equal to their grant. Examples include Rotary clubs, Kiwanis clubs, African American groups, and so on.

COLUMNS 2 THROUGH 10

The Grantseekers' Decision Matrix can be used in many ways. Vertical columns 2 through 10 provide information that will help you select the best type of funding source for your project. For example, if your problem and project are unique to your geographic area, you might look more closely at those funders whose primary concerns are local.

Your type of project may also be used to determine the most likely funder. For instance, is it a model project? Replication? Research? Equipment?

Another important variable related to your success is selecting the appropriate funder for your grant size or request. In other words, you wouldn't approach a small service club for full support of a project with a large grant request.

Your school's track record with grantors and who has invested in your school previously is also important, as is the image of the project director. Each type of funding source will look at the credentials of the project director differently. But name recognition and credibility are usually important to all.

Your ability to contact the prospective grantor, their proximity to you, and their expected protocols are also critical to choosing the "right" funder.

The required proposal content, review system used, and grants administration rules are variables that will give you an indication of how much time will be required of you and your grants committee in writing and administering your grant.

The next chapter will help you locate specific grantors within each type of funding source.

CHAPTER SEVEN

Researching Potential Funders

Your ultimate goal is to secure funding. To do this, you must develop a broad list of possible funders, eliminate the least likely prospects, and select the most likely. There are many resources right in your community to help you research potential funders — so many, in fact, that the number of potential funding sources you uncover could actually result in confusion. The key to finding the source most likely to fund you is to keep in mind the Values Approach to Grantseeking. In short, always remember to look at your grant idea from the point of view of the potential grantor. This means that you should define your project and its benefits from the grantor's viewpoint.

Computerized data bases and resource books are organized and indexed by subject area, geography, eligibility, and several other variables. Your success in utilizing these resource books and data bases will be a function of:

- your selection of research or key search words,

- the approaches or solutions you have developed, and

- your willingness to change or modify the solution to appeal to different types of funders.

Key Search Words

Many standard grants resources have a subject-area index. Subject areas such as child welfare, early childhood education, youth, and so on, can be thought of as key words. Under each category are listed all the funding sources that have expressed an interest in that area. Therefore, key words can help you *search* for potential funding sources. This is why they are called *key search words.*

When you begin your search for the best funding source for your project, start by determining the key words that can be related to your project. Also, think of ways you could change or adapt your project to relate to more key words or subject areas. The object is not merely to relate your project or idea to as many key words as possible but also to determine the ways it could be related to various funders' interests.

For example, say you are interested in using computers to teach reading to fourth graders. A particular funder may have an interest in literacy. If you define your project as one that is related to literacy, that particular funder will end up on your list of possible grantors. (Remember, not all the funders speak the same language that you do or have your vocabulary.)

The following Key Words Worksheets will help you look at your project/solution from the viewpoint of the funding source. The Key Words Worksheet for Government Grantseeking (Fig. 7.1) lists key words or descriptors that relate to federal programs dealing with the entire field of education as well as descriptors relating to programs dealing with elementary education only. The Key Words Worksheet for Foundation and Corporate Grantseeking (Fig. 7.2) lists many key words found in computer-assisted retrieval systems and reference books. Review the lists and designate those words that can be related to your project.

Searching for Funders

Armed with your key words, you are ready to initiate your search for funds. As you will see, you do not *need* to spend a lot on reference books or computer-based search systems. Many of these resources can be obtained inexpensively or for free. You may wish to start with a computer-assisted grants search.

How to Perform a Computer-assisted Grants Search

A. Check with your district's grants office to find out what computer assistance is available to you. Your school or district librarian may be able to help. Most libraries are linked to DIALOG, a data base of government and private funding sources, and they may carry out a search for you at no charge.

B. Invite a college or university faculty or staff member to be part of your grants advisory group. He or she should not be required to come to the meetings but should be willing to help you locate potential funders. Most colleges have a grants office, and even very small colleges often have computer-assisted search systems, such as the Sponsored Programs Information Network (SPIN) and the Illinois Research Information System (IRIS). Be sure to inform your potential college volunteer that you already have a list of *key words* for searching federal programs and private grantors (foundation and corporation). This will help to ensure a positive response.

Even if your district provides search services, I recommend that you include representatives of higher education in your grants process. The connection with a college or university provides you with:

- access to professional educators who have the credentials you may need to appeal to some funders,
- a different perspective for brainstorming that may lead to alternative solutions and ideas you would not have generated on your own,
- a possible consortium relationship and/or an alternative organization through which to submit your proposal,
- access to the inexpensive labor of graduate students,
- assistance in developing evaluation designs, statistical analysis, and data manipulation, and
- expertise with curriculum design.

Including a representative of higher education in your group does not mean that you are giving the project to her or him. You can maintain control over any components you wish to. Professors of education or related fields will usually be very willing to work with you because you can offer them:

KEY WORDS WORKSHEET
FOR GOVERNMENT GRANTSEEKING

The federal government uses the following subject index in describing grant opportunities in education. Review the list and indicate the key words that relate to your project. You may find it helpful to make a brief notation of any significant ways you could change your solution to make it relate to that key word.

The following descriptors relate to federal programs dealing with the whole area of education.

Adult Education
Disadvantaged Education
Early Childhood Education
Elementary Education
Health Education
Humanities Education
Indian Education
International Education
Tools for Schools

The following descriptors relate to federal programs dealing with elementary education.
Elementary Education Arts
Elementary Education Bilingual
Chapter 1
Chapter 2
Computer Learning
Disadvantaged/Deprived
Drug-Free Schools
Gifted and Talented Students
Handicapped
Homeless Children
Immigrant Children
Impact Aid
Math/Science
Migrant Education
Elementary Education Minorities
Neglected and Delinquent
Physical Fitness
Private Schools
School Dropout Prevention
Talent Search
Upward Bound

- access to your school and classroom,

- an opportunity to work with your students,

- extra income (if they work on a grant at their college, they get release time but not much extra cash compensation), and

- contact with elementary, middle, and junior high school teachers.

For the above reasons (plus their love for the field of education) you should be able to involve these fellow professionals in your project and get research into funding sources done on *their* computer data base.

Figure 7.2

KEY WORDS WORKSHEET FOR
FOUNDATION AND CORPORATE GRANTSEEKING

The following key words are utilized in many electronic data retrieval systems and printed reference books. Review the list and indicate the key words that relate to your project. You may find it helpful to make a brief notation of any significant ways you could change your solution to make it relate to that key word.

Adult/Continuing Education Programs
Alternative Modes/Nontraditional Study
Arts Education Programs
Bicultural/Bilingual Education Programs
Biological Sciences Education Programs
Business Education Programs
Career Education Programs
Children/Youth
Cognition/Information Processing
Communications Education Programs
Computer Science Education Programs
Computer Sciences
Computer-assisted Instruction
Conference Support
Early Childhood/Preschool Education
Educational Counseling/Guidance
Educational Reform
Educational Studies — Developing Countries
Educational Testing/Measurement
Educational Values
Elementary Education
Employment Opportunity Programs
Employment/Labor Studies
Energy Education Programs
English Education Programs
Environmental Studies Education Programs
Fine Arts Education Programs
Foreign Language Education Programs
Foreign Scholars
Gifted Children
Handicapped Education Services
Handicapped Vocational Services
Handicapped/Special Education Programs
Health Education Programs
Humanities Education Programs
Illiteracy
Information Dissemination
International Studies Education Programs
Journalism Education Programs
Learning Disorders/Dyslexia

Mathematics Education Programs
Minority Education Programs
Music Education Programs
Nutrition Education Programs
Opportunities Abroad
Parental Involvement in Education
Philosophy
Philosophy of Education
Physical Education Programs
Physical Sciences Education Programs
Precollegiate Education — Arts Education
    Programs
Precollegiate Education — Bilingual
    Education Programs
Precollegiate Education — Economics
    Education Programs
Precollegiate Education — Humanities
    Education Programs
Precollegiate Education — Professional
    Development
Precollegiate Education —
    Science/Math Education Programs
Prizes/Awards
Professional Development
Professional/Faculty Development
Reading Education Programs
Remedial Education
Rural Education
Rural Services
Rural Studies
Teacher Education
Telecommunications — Education
    Materials
Vocational/Technical Education
Women's Education Programs —
    Business Management
Women's Education Programs —
    Science/Engineering
Women's Studies Education Programs
Youth Employment Opportunity
    Programs

Government Grant Information Sources

Federal and state grants come from tax dollars and are therefore subject to many rules and to the Freedom of Information Act. This means that you have a right to free or inexpensive access to all information on federal grant opportunities. You should have a basic knowledge of the federal grants system even if your college advisory group member arranges a free search for you.

Government grant opportunities for education are available to your school either directly from federal programs or indirectly from federal programs passed through states. Some states develop their own grants programs, but there is no uniform mechanism for inviting applications for these funds. It is your responsibility to alert your building principal and district grants people of your interest in state grant opportunities. Since few states have grants systems as organized as the federal government's, you may find it helpful to check directly with your state education department. They can place you on their mailing list to send you information on their programs.

Direct federal grant opportunities are a different story. Since all prospective grantees must have an equal opportunity to learn about and apply for federal funds, there is a special system for the dissemination of federal grant information.

Ask educators in middle or elementary schools what that think of when they hear the words *federal grant opportunity* and chances are they many will describe scenes of confusion and panic. This is because in most school districts meeting a federal grants deadline is synonymous with last-minute, chaotic scrambling. Such panic is a result of reactive grantseeking. Elementary and middle school educators do not have to participate in this method of grantseeking. They *can* develop successful federal proposals and deal effectively with the pressure of deadlines by being knowledgeable about the federal grants process. I have been a consultant to several school districts seeking to develop an improved, *proactive* federal grants system. These districts now plot federal deadlines a year in advance and take advantage of all available resources to meet deadlines and even submit proposals early. In other words, they have developed a controlled approach to federal grantseeking.

The federal government grants over $75 billion each year. The grants system follows a yearly cycle. I refer to this cycle as the *Federal Grants Clock*.

Most federal grantseekers know that application packages are usually sent to prospective grantees four to eight weeks before the completed applications are due and that the grants are usually awarded four to six months after submission. The key to *proactive government grantseeking* is knowing *what else* occurs during the Federal Grants Clock and how your actions can dramatically increase your success rate while decreasing the madness associated with a last-minute rush to meet a deadline.

Do *not* wait to learn about a grant opportunity. Do *not* postpone preparing your proposal until you receive an application package. *Start early!* To do so, you need to have a working knowledge of the basic grant-information publications.

THE CATALOGUE OF FEDERAL DOMESTIC ASSISTANCE (CFDA)

In the fall of each year the federal government publishes *The Catalogue of Federal Domestic*

Assistance (CFDA). This catalogue lists the 1,225 granting programs that disseminate approximately $75 billion in grants annually and provides the grantseeker with all sorts of valuable information, including deadlines.

Figure 7.3

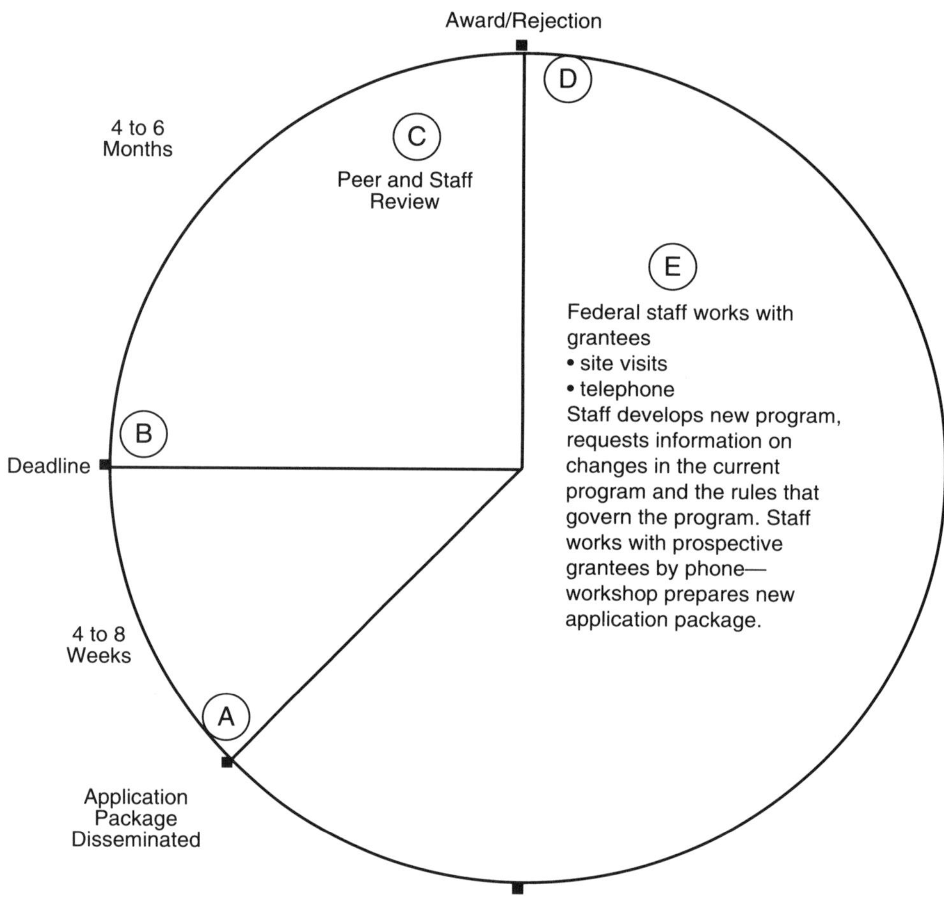

The clock operates 365 days per year. The federal government's year begins on October 1 and ends September 30.

Where Can You Get the CFDA? You may purchase the CFDA from the Superintendent of Documents, U.S. Government Printing Office, Washington, D.C. 20402 (202-783-3238) for under $50. However, you do not have to buy your own copy. The CFDA is provided free to at least two libraries in each congressional district. (Your congressperson should know which libraries have been designated Federal Depository Libraries.) Most public libraries also have copies, as do college and university libraries and grants offices.

Why Should You Use the CFDA? Even if you are planning to pursue only foundation or corporate grants, you should be knowledgeable about existing federal programs for your project area. Armed with this knowledge, you will be able to explain to a prospective private grantor why you are approaching them instead of a federal agency. For instance, if you *know for* *certain* that there are *no* federal program funds designated for your project area or that federal funding is limited to three projects across the entire country, it will be easier for you to demonstrate why private grant support is so necessary.

How Do You Use the CFDA? The most efficient way to locate the granting agencies that represent your best opportunities is to use the key words you circled on your Key Words Worksheets and compare them to the indexes in the CFDA. The CFDA has five indexes. However, the *Subject Index* is the most helpful index for locating grant opportunities in the Education Department and in other departments that have an interest in education.

In chapter 5 we discussed a project idea related to the use of parent-teacher-student contracts and videotape feedback. When searching for federal grant opportunities for this project, we used *resource development* and *support for elementary education* as our key words and looked for program matches in the CFDA's indexes. By looking in the Functional and the Subject indexes we matched our interests with several federal programs, including:

CFDA 84.201   School Dropout Demonstration Assistance

CFDA 84.212   First Family School Partnership

If we changed our project slightly and focused totally on math and science and parent-teacher-student contracts and videotape feedback we would yield other matches, such as CFDA 84.168, the National Program for Math and Science Education.

This book includes a sample of CFDA 84.201 to help you understand the federal grants system. This understanding is crucial to the development of a proactive grantseeking system that will enable you to start the process early and make preproposal contact with the appropriate funding agency.

In the example, CFDA 84.201 SCHOOL DROPOUT DEMONSTRATION ASSISTANCE — Dropout Prevention Program, reader aids have been numbered in the left margin and are in bold print in the text.

1. **Program Title:** School Dropout Demonstration Assistance (Dropout Prevention Program)

2. **Federal Agency:** This tells you the arm of the government that handles this program. While many of your grant programs will be sponsored by the Department of Education, you may also apply to the National Science Foundation, the National Endowment for the Arts, and so on.

3. **Authorization:** This tells you the source of the funding.

4. **Objectives:** This section is important because it gives you the first indication of the appropriateness of your idea in relationship to the funding program. In the example of a project to increase parent, teacher, and student responsibility, application to this program would be appropriate if the system was used as a model to keep children in school.

5. **Types of Assistance:** This program funds project grants. You must know what types of assistance are provided to determine if the federal program is interested in funding projects or research or if they fund on a formula basis that allocates the funds to eligible recipients through predetermined criteria.

6. **User and Use Restrictions:** User and use restrictions help you further determine if the program is an appropriate source of funds for your project. In this program, funds will be used to reduce the number of children who do not complete elementary education.

(1) 84.201 SCHOOL DROPOUT DEMONSTRATION ASSISTANCE
(Dropout Prevention Program)

(2) FEDERAL AGENCY: DEPARTMENT OF EDUCATION, OFFICE OF ELEMENTARY AND SECONDARY EDUCATION

(3) AUTHORIZATION: Elementary and Secondary Education Act of 1965, Title VI, Parts A and C, as amended, Public Law 100-297.

(4) OBJECTIVES: To provide financial assistance to local educational agencies, educational partnerships and community-based organizations to establish and demonstrate effective dropout prevention and reentry programs.

(5) TYPES OF ASSISTANCE: Project Grants.

(6) USES AND USE RESTRICTIONS: Funds may be used for activities directly related to reducing the number of children that do not complete their elementary and secondary education. Not more than five percent of any grant may be used for administrative costs. Local educational agencies (LEAs) must not use Federal funds to supplant funds that would, in the absence of Federal funds, be made available from nonfederal sources for the activities that assistance is being sought. The Federal share of grants under this program shall not exceed ninety percent of the total cost of a project for the first year and seventy-five percent of the cost for the second year. The nonfederal share may be paid from any other source. Not more than ten percent of the nonfederal share may be from other Federal sources. The nonfederal share may be in-cash or in-kind.

(7) ELIGIBILITY REQUIREMENTS:

Applicant Eligibility: Local educational agencies, community-based organizations, and educational partnerships may apply.

Beneficiary Eligibility: Student dropouts, institutions of higher education, students at-risk of dropping out, students reentering school, local educational agencies, State educational agencies, community-based organizations, business organizations and nonprofit organizations will benefit.

Credentials/Documentation: Costs will be determined in accordance with OMB Circular No. A-87 for State and local governments. OMB Circular No. A-122, Cost Principles for Nonprofit Organizations, also applies.

APPLICATION AND AWARD PROCESS:

Preapplication Coordination: The standard application forms as furnished by the Federal agency and required by OMB Circular No. A-102 must be used for this program. This program is eligible for coverage under E.O. 12372, "Intergovernmental Review of Federal Programs." An applicant should consult the office or official designated as the single contact point in his or her State for more information on the process the State requires to be followed in applying for assistance, if the State has selected the program for review.

(8) Application Procedure: Applications must be sent to the Department of Education on or before the closing date. This program is subject to the provisions of OMB Circular No. A-110.

Award Procedure: Recommendations for the approval of applications are made by the program staff on the basis of published criteria, statutory considerations, and with the advice and assistance of a panel of expert reviewers. Applications are approved for awards by the Assistant Secretary for Elementary and Secondary Education, after completion of the competitive review.

Deadlines: Established by notice published in the Federal Register.

Range of Approval/Disapproval Time: The closing date will be published in the Federal Register.

Appeals: None.

Renewals: A grant recipient is eligible for continuation of its award for up to three additional years if it meets the criteria for continuation.

(9) ASSISTANCE CONSIDERATIONS:

Formula and Matching Requirements: The Federal share under this program shall not exceed 90 percent of the total project costs for the first year and 75 percent of the cost for the second year.

Length and Time Phasing of Assistance: Approximately twelve months.

(10) POST ASSISTANCE REQUIREMENTS:

Reports: Annual performance and financial reports are required in accordance with the provisions of EDGAR, Section 75.720.

Audits: In accordance with the provisions of OMB Circular No. A-128, "Audits of State and Local Governments," State and local governments that receive financial assistance of $100,000 or more within the State's fiscal year shall have an audit made for that year. State and local governments that receive between $25,000 and $100,000 within the State's fiscal year shall have an audit made in accordance with Circular No. A-128, or in accordance with Federal laws and regulations governing the programs in which they participate.

Records: In accordance with Education Department General Administrative Regulations, 34 CFR 74 and 75.

(11) FINANCIAL INFORMATION:

Account Identification: 91-1000-0-1-501

Obligations: (Grants) FY 90 $19,945,000; FY 91 est $32,600,000; and FY 92 est $27,214,000.

Range and Average of Financial Assistance: For fiscal year 1991, the range is estimated to be from $250,000 to $1,500,000; $694,000.

(12) PROGRAM ACCOMPLISHMENTS: In fiscal year 1990, 89 continuation grants were awarded: fourteen to local educational agencies (LEAs) and five to educational partnerships in LEAs with enrollments of 100,000 or more students; twenty-one to LEAs and eight to educational partnerships in LEAs with enrollments of 20,000 to 99,999 students; twenty-seven to LEAs and seven to educational partnerships with enrollments of less than 20,000 students; and seven to community-based organizations. New grants will be awarded in fiscal year 1991.

(13) **REGULATIONS, GUIDELINES, AND LITERATURE:** The Department of Education, General Administrative Regulations (EDGAR); 34 CFR 74, Administration of Grants, Part 75, Direct Grant Programs, Part 77, Definitions that Apply to Department Regulations, Part 79 (Intergovernmental Review of Department of Education Programs and Activities), Part 80 (Uniform Administrative Requirements for Grants and Cooperative Agreements with State and Local Governments), Part 81 (General Education Provisions Act-Enforcement), Part 82 (New Restrictions on Lobbying), Part 85 (Governmentwide Debarment and Suspension (non-procurement) and Governmentwide Requirements for Drug-Free Workplace (grants) and Pact 86 (Drug-Free Schools and Campuses).

(14) **INFORMATION CONTACTS:**

Regional or Local Office: Not applicable.

Headquarters Office: Department of Education, Division of Educational Support, Office of Elementary and Secondary Education, 400 Maryland Avenue, SW., Mail Stop 624, Washington, DC 20202-6438. Contact: John R. Fiegel. Telephone: (202) 401-1342.

(15) **RELATED PROGRAMS:** None.

(16) **EXAMPLES OF FUNDED PROJECTS:** Grantees replicate or expand successful programs designed to: identify potential student dropouts, and keep them from dropping out; identify and encourage children that have already dropped out to reenter school; identify at-risk students in elementary and secondary schools; and establish model systems for collecting and reporting information. Typical activities include developing and implementing an extended day, or summer programs designed to address poor achievement, basic skills deficiencies, or course failures; establishing or expanding work-study, apprentice, or internship programs; training school staff; training parents in the use of community services; improving student motivation and the school learning environment; providing alternative classrooms and alternative schools, and other educational, occupational, and testing services intended to reduce the number of dropouts. Grantees will be required to cooperate with a national evaluation study. In fiscal year 1991, priority will be given to restructuring and reform projects and comprehensive targeted programs for at-risk youth.

(17) **CRITERIA FOR SELECTING PROPOSALS:** The Secretary evaluates applications on the basis of criteria required under EDGAR (Parts 75, 76, and 77).

7. Eligibility Requirements:

- Applicant Eligibility — This section tells you if your school is an eligible recipient. Your school is designated as a Local Educational Agency (LEA). If your school is not eligible for funding under this program, this section will tell you whom you should develop a relationship with to submit your proposal through that organization.

- Beneficiary Eligibility — This section tells you what type of individual or organization is intended to benefit from the project.

- Credentials/Documentation — The Office of Management and Budget (OMB) publishes several management booklets that outline the rules for requesting, spending, and documenting expenditures under a federal grant.

8. Application and Award Process:

- Preapplication Coordination — This section outlines the OMB requirements related to your state's review and knowledge of your proposal. If you have a district grants office, they will know whom to contact in your state office concerning this matter.

- Application Procedure — This describes the rules for submittal.

- Award Procedure — This section tells you who will review and approve your proposal. Proposals submitted to this particular program will be read by program staff based on the published criteria. Although experts will also read the proposals and assist the staff members, in this example your writing style and level should be in accordance with the background of the staff.

- Deadlines — Established by notice published in *The Federal Register. The Federal Register* is explained immediately following this CFDA example.

- Range of Approval/Disapproval Time — Closing date published in *The Federal Register.*
- Appeals — In this case, there is no procedure for appealing the grantor's decision. Some federal programs have a specific appeal procedure.
- Renewals — This information is important when you are planning a project that may take several years. In this case, a grant recipient is eligible for continuation of its award for up to three years if it meets the criteria.

9. **Assistance Considerations:**

- Formula and Matching Requirements — This section outlines what portion of the project costs will be borne by your school district. It is vital that you have a plan for the match and your school's endorsement that it will commit this share. In this example, the recipient would need *at least* a 10 percent match in year one and a 25 percent match in year two.
- Length and Time Phasing of Assistance — In this case, approximately 12 months.

10. **Post-Assistance Requirements:** Your district will be required to make reports and maintain records and may be subject to audits. Don't let this section scare you. Your business office will handle it.

11. **Financial Information:**

- Account Identification — Account identification number.
- Obligations — By reviewing this section, you can determine if the program is slated to increase or decrease its funding level. Note: It is estimated that the future budget for this program will be $27,214,000, but this figure could be changed drastically by Congress. In this example, program funds went up, then down.
- Range and Average of Financial Assistance — In 1991 the range was $250,000 to $1,500,000, with the average award being $694,000. This should indicate to you that this program is not your best choice if you are requesting $25,000 per year.

12. **Program Accomplishments:** This section gives you important information on previously selected grantees and on the number of awards made in the past. In this case, 89 awards were divided up by size of district in 1990. This section will also inform you if the program is being phased out. For example, it may say "no new awards."

13. **Regulations, Guidelines, and Literature:** This section outlines the rules and guidelines. Most of the rules mentioned pertain to your district personnel and business office. The only one that is relatively new is the Drug-Free Workplace and Campus rule. Compliance should be discussed with your district grants office or administration.

14. **Information Contacts:**

- Regional or Local Office — Most regional offices were closed during the federal cutbacks of the early 1980s.
- Headquarters Office — This section provides the contact name, address, and phone number you will need if you select this funder as a possible source of funds for your project.

15. **Related Programs:** This section lists the CFDA names and digit codes of other sources of funds that have similar target populations and/or objectives.

16. **Examples of Funded Projects:** This section provides a sample of the solutions that the grantor valued highly enough to fund.

17. **Criteria for Selecting Proposals:** This section lists the types of criteria that the agency will follow in the evaluation procedures. Each agency has its own criteria, and criteria may differ between programs. The criterion used in this example is EDGAR (parts 75, 76, and 77), which will be discussed in chapter 12, "Improving and Submitting Your Federal Grant Application."

THE FEDERAL REGISTER

The Federal Register is the federal government's daily newspaper. From a teacher's perspective, this resource could cause a severe case of cognitive overload. You should not read this publication on a daily basis. You just need to know what its purpose is as it relates to federal grantseeking.

The Federal Register provides the government with a way to solicit feedback on the rules that governed the previous year's grant solicitation and award process. It is not unusual for the federal agency to publish the previous year's rules in *The Federal Register* six months before the next deadline to solicit the public's opinions on the way the proposals are awarded.

A period of 30 days is usually given to comment on the rules. The agency reviews the comments and may make changes based on them. The public is then allowed another 30 days to comment on the changes before the *final rules* are printed. These rules will govern the program's priorities and the scoring or review system; they also provide valuable insight into exactly what the agency is looking for.

Being aware of this process gives you a strong advantage over your competitors. You now know that there is no need to wait around until you receive a formal application package. You know that you can telephone a federal program officer to ask when information on the rules and the deadline was printed in *The Federal Register.* The information you obtain from the CFDA and *The Federal Register* enables you to make a decision on the appropriateness of the funding opportunity, and you can get started!

You can use your new knowledge concerning the two most basic federal grants publications, the CFDA and *The Federal Register,* to look like a "grants pro." For example, assume that you have used your key words and the CFDA indexes to determine that CFDA 84.201, the School Dropout Demonstration Assistance Program, looks like a good potential funding source for your project. You could contact John Fiegel, the information contact listed in the CFDA, to ask if the deadline has been announced yet and if it hasn't, when he thinks it will appear in *The Federal Register.* You could also ask him if any notices have been published in the Register that could assist you, such as comments on the rules, and so on.

If, for example, you contacted Mr. Fiegel in December, he may have informed you that the notice to invite applicants was to be printed in January and that the application deadline was expected to be March. Clearly, you would be a step ahead of your competitors and gain significant insight by obtaining a copy of the January *Federal Register.*

You must know the exact day that the rules were printed. In this case, it was January 17. Frequently the federal agency will reproduce this *Federal Register* and include it in the application package in March.

Now that you are familiar with one CFDA program, you are aware of the indexes and the format in which descriptions of all 1,225 federal programs appear in *The Catalogue of Federal Domestic Assistance.*

The CFDA is also available in electronic form. This makes searching for federal programs faster and the information more accessible to rural nonprofit organizations that may be a considerable distance from a Federal Depository Library.

The computerized version of the CFDA is known as the Federal Assistance Program Retrieval System, or FAPRS. You can usually obtain a FAPRS search by locating the state agency designated to provide such searches. You may be asked to pay a small fee, or the service may be free. To locate your nearest access point, write or call:

The Federal Domestic Assistance Catalogue Staff (WKU)
General Services Administration
Ground Floor, Reporters Building
300 7th Street, S.W.
Washington, DC 20407
Telephone (202) 708-5126
Toll Free Answering Service 1-800-669-8331

There are also several commercially available software programs. While you can purchase the FAPRS discs from the Catalogue staff for $140, you may find that by paying slightly more you can get a more "user-friendly" version. For instance, GRANTSEARCH CFDA is available from Capitol Publications, Inc., P.O. Box 1453, Alexandria, VA 22313 - 2053 (1-800-847-7772). It was priced at $425 at the time of this printing.

Information on computer-search resources containing both federal and private funding sources (foundation and corporate) can be found in the bibliography.

Foundation Research Tools

The Foundation Center Library National Collections offer the best available selection of information on foundation and corporate grants. The National Collections are located in New York City, Washington, D.C., Cleveland, and San Francisco. To help nonprofit organizations that are not able to access the National Collections, cooperating collections have been established in libraries, community foundations, and even some nonprofit agencies throughout the United States. The organizations that house the cooperating collections do not get paid to do so, although they do receive the publications for free. Use the following list to locate the collection nearest you and take advantage of its many reference books on foundation funding.

The most useful book will be a foundation book that focuses on your state. Most states have a state directory, which you can find at your cooperating collection.

The Foundation Center publishes several popular grants reference materials, including *The Foundation Directory.* Available at your Foundation Center Regional Library, this yearly publication is the most important single reference work on grant-making foundations in the United States. The 1993 edition will be the fifteenth. To be included in the *Directory,* a foundation must either have assets of at least $2 million or make grants in excess of $200,000

THE FOUNDATION CENTER COOPERATING COLLECTIONS NETWORK
Free Funding Information Centers

The Foundation Center is an independent national service organization established by foundations to provide an authoritative source of information on private philanthropic giving. The New York, Washington, DC, Cleveland and San Francisco reference collections operated by the Foundation Center offer a wide variety of services and comprehensive collections of information on foundations and grants. Cooperating Collections are libraries, community foundations and other nonprofit agencies that provide a core collection of Foundation Center publications and a variety of supplementary materials and services in areas useful to grantseekers. The core collection consists of:

Foundation Directory 1 and 2	Foundation Grants to Individuals	National Directory of Corporate Giving
Foundation Fundamentals	Literature of the Nonprofit Sector	Source Book Profiles
Foundation Grants Index	National Data Book of Foundations	User-Friendly Guide
Foundation Grants Index Quarterly		

Many of the network members have sets of private foundation information returns (IRS 990-PF) for their state or region which are available for public use. A complete set of U.S. foundation returns can be found at the New York and Washington, DC, offices of the Foundation Center. The Cleveland and San Francisco offices contain IRS 990-PF returns for the midwestern and western states, respectively. Those Cooperating Collections marked with a bullet (•) have sets of private foundation information returns for their state or region.

Because the collections vary in their hours, materials and services, IT IS RECOMMENDED THAT YOU CALL EACH COLLECTION IN ADVANCE. To check on new locations or more current information, call 1-800-424-9836.

Reference Collections Operated by the Foundation Center

The Foundation Center	The Foundation Center	The Foundation Center	The Foundation Center
8th Floor	Room 312	1001 Connecticut Avenue, NW	Kent H. Smith Library
79 Fifth Avenue	312 Sutter Street	Washington, DC 20036	1422 Euclid, Suite 1356
New York, NY 10003	San Francisco, CA 94108	202-331-1400	Cleveland, OH 44115
212-620-4230	415-397-0902		216-861-1933

ALABAMA

•Birmingham Public Library
Government Documents
2100 Park Place
Birmingham 35203
205-620-3600

Huntsville Public Library
915 Monroe St.,
Huntsville 35801
205-532-5940

University of South Alabama
Library Reference Dept.
Mobile 36688
205-460-7025

•Auburn University at
Montgomery Library
7300 University Drive
Montgomery 36117-3596
205-244-3653

ALASKA

•University of Alaska Anchorage
Library
3211 Providence Drive
Anchorage 99508
907-786-1848

Juneau Public Library
292 Marine Way
Juneau 99801
907-586-5249

ARIZONA

•Phoenix Public Library
Business & Sciences Dept.
12 East McDowell Road
Phoenix 85257
602-262-4636

•Tucson Public Library
101 N. Stone Ave.
Tucson 85726-7470
602-791-4393

ARKANSAS

•Westark Community
College Library

5210 Grand Avenue
Fort Smith 72913
501-785-7000

Central Arkansas Library System
Reference Services
700 Louisiana Street
Little Rock 72201
501-370-5950

Pine Bluff-Jefferson County
Library System
200 East Eighth
Pine Bluff 71601
501-534-2159

CALIFORNIA

Ventura County
Community Foundation
Community Resource Center
1357 Del Norte Road
Camarillo 93010
805-988-0196

•Orange County Community
Developmental Council
1695 W. MacArthur Blvd.
Costa Mesa 92626
714-540-9293

•California Community
Foundation
Funding Information Center
606 S. Olive St., Suite 2400
Los Angeles 90014-1526
213-413-4042

•Community Foundation for
Monterey County
177 Van Buren
Monterey 93942
408-375-9712

Riverside Public Library
3581 7th Street
Riverside 92501
714-782-5201

California State Library
Reference Services, Rm. 301
914 Capitol Mall

Sacramento 94237-0001
916-322-4570

Nonprofit Resource Center
Sacramento Central Library
Downtown Plaza South Mall
Sacramento 95812-2036
916-449-2131

•San Diego Community
Foundation
101 W. Broadway, Suite 1120
San Diego 92101
619-239-8815

•Nonprofit Development
Center
1762 Technology Dr., Suite 225
San Jose 95110
408-452-8181

•Peninsula Community
Foundation
1700 S. El Camino Real
San Mateo 94402-3049
415-358-9392

Volunteer Center Resource
Library
1000 E. Santa Ana Blvd.
Santa Ana 92701
714-953-1655

•Santa Barbara Public Library
40 East Anapamu
Santa Barbara 93101-1603
805-962-7653

Santa Monica Public
Library
1343 Sixth Street
Santa Monica 90401-1603
213-458-8600

COLORADO

Pikes Peak Library District
20 North Cascade Avenue
Colorado Springs 80901
719-473-2080

•Denver Public Library
Sociology Division

1357 Broadway
Denver 80203
303-640-8870

CONNECTICUT

Danbury Public Library
170 Main Street
Danbury 06810
203-797-4527

•Hartford Public Library
Reference Department
500 Main Street
Hartford 06103
203-293-6000

D.A.T. A.
70 Audubon St.
New Haven 06510
203-772-1345

DELAWARE

•University of Delaware
Hugh Morris Library
Newark 19717-5267
302-451-2432

FLORIDA

Volusia County Library Center
City Island
Daytona Beach 32014-4484
904-255-3765

•Nova University
Einstein Library ——
Foundation Resource
Collection
3301 College Avenue
Fort Lauderdale 33314
305-475-7497

Indian River Community
College
Learning Resources Center
3209 Virginia Avenue
Fort Pierce 34981-5599
407-468-4757

•Jacksonville Public Libraries
Business, Science &

Documents
122 North Ocean Street
Jacksonville 32206
904-630-2665

•Miami-Dade Public Library
Humanities Department
101 W. Flagler St.
Miami 33130
305-375-2665

•Orlando Public Library
Orange County Library System
101 E. Central Blvd.
Orlando 32801
407-425-4694

Selby Public Library
1001 Boulevard of the Arts
Sarasota 34236
813-951-5501

•Leon County Public Library
Funding Resource Center
200 W. Park Ave.
Tallahassee 32301
904-487-2665

Tampa Hillsborough County
 Public Library System
900 N. Ashley Drive
Tampa 33602
813-223-8866

Community Foundation of
 Palm Beach and Martin
 Counties
324 Datura Street
West Palm Beach 33401
407-659-6800

GEORGIA

•Atlanta-Fulton Public Library
Foundation Collection —
 Ivan Allen Department
1 Margaret Mitchell Square
Atlanta 30303-1089
404-730-1900

HAWAII

•Hawaii Community Foundation
Hawaii Resource Room
222 Merchant Street
Honolulu 96813
808-537-6333

University of Hawaii
Thomas Hale Hamilton Library
2550 The Mall
Honolulu 96822
808-956-7214

IDAHO

•Boise Public Library
715 S. Capitol Blvd.
Boise 83702
208-384-4024

•Caldwell Public Library
1010 Dearborn Street
Caldwell 83605
208-459-3242

ILLINOIS

Belleville Public Library
121 East Washington St.
Belleville 62220
618-234-0441

•Donors Forum of Chicago
53 W. Jackson Blvd., Rm. 430

Chicago 60604
312-431-0265

•Evanston Public Library
1703 Orrington Avenue
Evanston 60201
708-866-0305

•Sangamon State University
 Library
Shepherd Road
Springfield 62794-9243
217-786-6633

INDIANA

•Allen County Public Library
900 Webster Street
Fort Wayne 46802
219-424-7241

Indiana University Northwest
 Library
3400 Broadway
Gary 46408
219-980-6582

•Indianapolis-Marion County
 Public Library
40 East St. Clair Street
Indianapolis 46206
317-269-1733

IOWA

•Cedar Rapids Public Library
Funding Information Center
500 First Street, SE
Cedar Rapids 52401
319-398-5123

•Southwestern Community
 College
Learning Resource Center
1501 W. Townline Rd.
Creston 50801
515-782-7081, ext. 262

•Public Library of Des Moines
100 Locust Street
Des Moines 50308
515-283-4152

KANSAS

•Topeka Public Library
1515 West Tenth Street
Topeka 66604
913-233-2040

•Wichita Public Library
223 South Main
Wichita 67202
316-262-0611

KENTUCKY

Western Kentucky University
Helm-Cravens Library
Bowling Green 42101
502-745-6125

•Louisville Free Public Library
301 York St.
Louisville 40203
502-561-8617

LOUISIANA

•East Baton Rouge Parish Library
Centroplex Branch
120 St. Louis Street
Baton Rouge 70802
504-389-4960

•Beauregard Parish Library
205 S. Washington Ave.

De Ridder 70634
318-463-6217

•New Orleans Public Library
Business and Science Division
219 Loyola Avenue
New Orleans 70140
504-596-2580

•Shreve Memorial Library
424 Texas Street
Shreveport 71120-1523
318-226-5894

MAINE

•University of Southern Main
Office of Sponsored Research
246 Deering Ave., Rm. 628
Portland 04103
207-780-4871

MARYLAND

•Enoch Pratt Free Library
Social Science and History
 Department
400 Cathedral Street
Baltimore 21201
301-396-5320

Carroll County Public Library
Government and Funding
Information Center
50 E. Main St.
Westminster 21157
301-848-4250

MASSACHUSETTS

•Associated Grantmakers of
 Massachusett
294 Washington Street
Suite 840
Boston 02108
617-426-2608

•Boston Public Library
666 Boylston St.
Boston 02117
617-536-5400

Western Massachusetts Funding
 Resource Center
Campaign for Human
 Development
65 Elliot St.
Springfield 01101
413-732-3175

•Worcester Public Library
Grants Resource Center
Salem Square
Worcester 01608
508-799-0655

MICHIGAN

•Alpena County Library
211 North First Avenue
Alpena 49707
517-356-6188

University of Michigan —— Ann
 Arbor
209 Hatcher Graduate Library
Ann Arbor 48109-1205
313-764-1148

•Battle Creek Community
 Foundation
One Riverwalk Centre
34 W. Jackson St.
Battle Creek 49017
616-962-2181

•Henry Ford Centennial Library
16301 Michigan Avenue
Dearborn 48126
313-943-2330

•Wayne State University
Purdy-Kresge Library
5265 Cass Avenue
Detroit 48202
313-577-6424

•Michigan State University
 Libraries
Reference Library
East Lansing 48824-1048
517-353-8818

•Farmington Community Library
32737 West 12 Mile Road
Farmington Hills 48018
313-553-0300

•University of Michigan —— Flint
 Library
Reference Department
Flint 48502-2186
313-762-3408

•Grand Rapids Public Library
Business Dept.
60 Library Plaza NE
Grand Rapids 49503-3093
616-456-3600

•Michigan Technological
 University Library
1400 Townsend Dr.
Houghton 49931
906-487-2507

•Sault Ste. Marie Area Public
 Schools
Office of Compensatory
 Education
460 W. Spruce St.
Sault Ste. Marie 49783-1874
906-635-6619

MINNESOTA

•Duluth Public Library
520 W. Superior Street
Duluth 55802
218-723-3802

Southwest State University
 Library
Marshall 56258
507-537-7278

•Minneapolis Public Library
Sociology Department
300 Nicollet Mall
Minneapolis 55401
612-372-6555

Rochester Public Library
11 First Street, SE
Rochester 55902-3743
507-285-8000

St. Paul Public Library
90 West Fourth Street
Saint Paul 55102
612-292-6307

MISSISSIPPI

Jackson —— Hinds Library
 System
300 North State Street
Jackson 39201
601-968-5803

MISSOURI

•Clearinghouse for Midcontinent
 Foundations
Univ. of Missouri
Block School of Business
5110 Cherry St., Suite 310
Kansas City 64112
816-235-1176

•Kansas City Public Library
311 East 12th Street
Kansas City 64106
816-221-9650

•Metropolitan Association for
 Philanthropy, Inc.
5585 Pershing Avenue
Suite 150
St. Louis 63112
314-361-3900

•Springfield —— Greene County
 Library
397 East Central Street
Springfield 65801
417-866-4636

MONTANA

•Eastern Montana College Library
1500 N. 30th Street
Billings 59101-0298
406-657-1662

Bozeman Public Library
220 East Lamme
Bozeman 59715-3579
406-586-4787

•Montana State Library
Reference Department
1515 E. 6th Avenue
Helena 59620
406-444-3004

NEBRASKA

•University of Nebraska
106 Love Library
14th & R Streets
Lincoln 68588-0410
402-472-2848

•W. Dale Clark Library
Social Sciences Department
215 South 15th Street
Omaha 68102
402-444-4826

NEVADA

•Las Vegas —— Clark County
 Library District
1401 East Flamingo Road
Las Vegas 89119-6160
702-733-7810

•Washoe County Library
301 South Center Street
Reno 89501
702-785-4012

NEW HAMPSHIRE

•New Hampshire Charitable Fund
One South Street
Concord 03302-1335
603-225-6641

•Plymouth State College
Herbert H. Lamson Library
Plymouth 03264
603-535-2258

NEW JERSEY

Cumberland County Library
800 E. Commerce Street
Bridgeton 08302-2295
609-453-2210

The Support Center
17 Academy Street, Suite 1101
Newark 07102
201-643-5774

County College of Morris
Masten Learning Resource
 Center
Route 10 and Center Grove Rd.
Randolph 07869
201-328-5296

•New Jersey State Library
Governmental Reference
185 West State Street
Trenton 08625-0520
609-292-6220

NEW MEXICO

Albuquerque Community
 Foundation
6400 Uptown Boulevard N.E.
Albuquerque 87105
505-883-6240

•New Mexico State Library
325 Don Gaspar Street
Santa Fe 87503
505-827-3824

NEW YORK

•New York State Library
Cultural Education Center
Humanities Section
Empire State Plaza
Albany 12230
518-474-5355

Suffolk Cooperative Library System
627 North Sunrise Service Road
Bellport 11713
516-286-1600

New York Public Library
Bronx Reference Center
2556 Bainbridge Avenue
Bronx 10458
212-220-6575

Brooklyn in Touch
One Hanson Place
Room 2504
Brooklyn 11243
718-230-3200

•Buffalo and Erie County Public
 Library
Lafayette Square
Buffalo 14202
716-858-7103

Huntington Public Library
338 Main Street
Huntington 11743
516-427-5165

Queens Borough Public Library
89-11 Merrick Boulevard
Jamaica 11432
718-990-0700

•Levittown Public Library
One Bluegrass Lane
Levittown 11756
516-731-5728
SUNY/College at Old Westbury
 Library

223 Store Hill Road
Old Westbury 11568
516-876-3156

Adriance Memorial Library
93 Market Street
Poughkeepsie 12601
914-485-3445

•Rochester Public Library
Business Division
115 South Avenue
Rochester 14604
716-428-7328

•Onondaga County Public Library
 at the Galleries
447 S. Salina Street
Syracuse 13202-2494
315-448-4636

•White Plains Public Library
100 Martine Avenue
White Plains 10601
914-422-1480

NORTH CAROLINA

•Asheville-Buncomb Technical
Community College
Learning Resources Center
340 Victoria Rd.
Asheville 28802
704-254-1921 ext. 300

•The Duke Endowment
200 S. Tryon Street, Ste. 1100
Charlotte 28202
704-376-0291

Durham County Library
300 N. Roxboro Street
Durham 27702
919-560-0100

•North Carolina State Library
109 East Jones Street
Raleigh 27611
919-733-3270

•The Winston-Salem Foundation
310 W. 4th St., Suite 229
Winston-Salem 27101-2889
919-725-2382

NORTH DAKOTA

•North Dakota State University
The Library
Fargo 58105
701-237-8886

OHIO

Stark County District Library
715 Market Avenue North
Canton 44702-1080
216-452-0665

•Public Library of Cincinnati and
 Hamilton County
Education Department
800 Vine Street
Cincinnati 45202-2071
513-369-6940

Columbus Metropolitan Library
96 S. Grant Avenue
Columbus 43215
614-645-2590

•Dayton and Montgomery County
 Public Library
Grants Information Center
215 E. Third Street
Dayton 45402-2103

513-227-9500 ext. 211

Toledo — Lucas County Public
 Library
Social Science Department
325 Michigan Street
Toledo 43623-1614
419-259-5245

Ohio University ——Zanesville
Community Education and
Development
1425 Newark Road
Zanesville 43701
614-453-0762

OKLAHOMA

•Oklahoma City University Library
2501 North Blackwelder
Oklahoma City 73106
405-521-5072

Tulsa City — County Library
 System
400 Civic Center
Tulsa 74103
918-596-7944

OREGON

Oregon Institute of Technology
 Library
3201 Campus Dr.
Klamath Falls 97601-8801
503-885-1772

•Pacific Non-Profit Network
Grantsmanship Resource Library
33 N. Central, Ste. 211
Medford 97501
503-779-6044

•Multnomah County Library
Government Documents Room
801 S.W. Tenth Avenue
Portland 97205-2597
503-248-5123

Oregon State Library
State Library Building
Salem 97310
503-378-4277

PENNSYLVANIA

Northampton Community College
Learning Resources Center
3835 Green Pond Road
Bethlehem 18017
215-861-5360

•Erie County Public Library
3 South Perry Square
Erie 16501
814-451-6927

Dauphin County Library System
101 Walnut Street
Harrisburg 17101
717-234-4961

Lancaster County Public Library
125 North Duke Street
Lancaster 17602
717-394-2651

•The Free Library of Philadelphia
Logan Square
Philadelphia 19103
215-686-5423

•University of Pittsburgh
Hillman Library
Pittsburgh 15260
412-648-7722

Economic Development Council
of Northeastern Pennsylvania
1151 Oak Street
Pittston 18640
717-655-5581

RHODE ISLAND

Providence Public Library
Reference Department
150 Empire St.
Providence 02903
401-521-7722

SOUTH CAROLINA

•Charleston County Library
404 King Street
Charleston 29403
803-723-1645

South Carolina State Library
Reference Department
1500 Senate Street
Columbia 29211
803-734-8666

SOUTH DAKOTA

Nonprofit Grants Assistance
Center
Business and Education Institute,
East Hall
Dakota State University
Madison 57042
605-256-5555

•South Dakota State Library
800 Governors Drive
Pierre 57501-2294
605-773-5070
800-592-1841 (SD residents)

Sioux Falls Area Foundation
141 N. Main Ave., Suite 500
Sioux Falls 57102-1134
605-336-7055

TENNESSEE

•Knoxville —Knox County
Public Library
500 West Church Avenue
Knoxville 37902
615-544-5750

•Memphis & Shelby County
Public Library
1850 Peabody Avenue
Memphis 38104
901-725-8877

•Public Library of Nashville and
Davidson County
8th Ave. N. and Union St.
Nashville 37203
615-259-6256

TEXAS

•Community Foundation of
Abilene
Funding Information Library
500 N. Chestnut, Suite 1509

Abilene 79604
915-676-3883

Amarillo Area Foundation
700 1st National Place One
800 S. Fillmore
Amarillo 79101
806-376-4521

•Hogg Foundation for Mental
Health
University of Texas
Austin 78713-7998
512-471-5041

•Corpus Christi State University
Library
6300 Ocean Drive
Corpus Christi 78412
512-994-2608

•Dallas Public Library
Grants Information Service
1515 Young Street
Dallas 75201
215-670-1487

•Pan American University
Learning Resource Center
1201 W. University Drive
Edinburg 78539
512-381-3304

•El Paso Community Foundation
1616 Texas Commerce Building
El Paso 79901
915-533-4020

•Texas Christian University
Library
Funding Information Center
Ft. Worth 76129
817-921-7664

•Houston Public Library
Bibliographic Information Center
500 McKinney Avenue
Houston 77002
713-236-1313

Lubbock Area Foundation
502 Texas Commerce Bank
Building
Lubbock 79401
806-762-8061

•Funding Information Center
507 Brooklyn
San Antonio 78215
512-227-4333

UTAH

•Salt Lake City Public Library
Business and Science Dept.
209 East Fifth South
Salt Lake City 84111
801-363-5733

VERMONT

•Vermont Dept. of Libraries
Reference Services

109 State Street
Montpelier 05609
802-828-3268

VIRGINIA

•Hampton Public Library
Grants Resources Collection
4207 Victoria Blvd.
Hampton 23669
804-727-1154

•Richmond Public Library
Business, Science, & Technology
101 East Franklin Street
Richmond 23219
804-780-8223

•Roanoke City Public Library
System
Central Library
706 S. Jefferson Street
Roanoke 24016
703-981-2477

WASHINGTON

•Seattle Public Library
1000 Fourth Avenue
Seattle 98104
206-386-4620

•Spokane Public Library
Funding Information Center
West 906 Main Avenue
Spokane 99201
509-838-3364

Greater Wenatchee Community
Foundation at the Wenatchee
Public Library
310 Douglas St.
Wenatchee 98807
509-662-5021

WEST VIRGINIA

•Kanawha County Public Library
123 Capital Street
Charleston 25304
304-343-4646

WISCONSIN

•University of Wisconsin —
Madison
Memorial Library
728 State Street
Madison 53706
608-262-3242

•Marquette University Memorial
Library
1415 West Wisconsin Avenue
Milwaukee 53233
414-288-1515

WYOMING

•Laramie County Community
College Library
1400 East College Drive
Cheyenne 82007-3299
307-778-1205

Teton County Library
Community Resource Library
320 S. King St.
Jackson 83001
307-733-2164

AUSTRALIA

ANZ Executors & Trustees Co.
Ltd.
91 William St., 7th floor
Melbourne VIC 3000
03-648-5764

CANADA

Canadian Centre for Philanthropy
1329 Bay St., Suite 200
Toronto, Ontario M5R 2C4
416-515-0764

ENGLAND

Charities Aid Foundation
114/118 Southampton Row
London WC1B 5AA
71-831-7798

JAPAN

Foundation Library Center of
Japan
Elements Shinjuku Bldg. 3F
2-1-14 Shinjuku, Shinjuku-ku
Tokyo 160
03-350-1857

MEXICO

Biblioteca Benjamin Franklin
American Embassy, USICA
Londres 16
Mexico City 6, D.F. 06600
905-211-0042

PUERTO RICO

University of Puerto Rico
Ponce Technological College
Library
Box 7186
Ponce 00732
809-844-8181

Universidad Del Sagrado
Corazon
M.M.T. Guevarra Library
Correo Calle Loiza
Santurce 00914
809-728-1515 ext. 357

U.S. VIRGIN ISLANDS

University of the Virgin Islands
Paiewonsky Library
Charlotte Amalie
St. Thomas 00802
809-776-9200

Participants in the Cooperating Collections Network are libraries or nonprofit information centers that provide fundraising information or other funding-related technical assistance in their communities. Cooperating Collections agree to provide free public access to a basic collection of Foundation Center publications during a regular schedule of hours, offering free funding research guidance to all visitors. Many also provide a variety of special services for local nonprofit organizations, using staff or volunteers to prepare special materials, organize workshops, or conduct library orientations.

The Foundation Center welcomes inquiries from libraries or information centers in the U.S.A. interested in providing this type of public information service. If you are interested in establishing a funding information library for the use of nonprofit agencies in your area or in learning more about the program, please write to: Anne J. Borland, The Foundation Center, 79 Fifth Avenue, New York, NY 10003.

annually. Over 6,300 of the existing 33,000 foundations have met at least one of these criteria and are include in the *Directory.*

The Foundation Directory, Part 2: A Guide to Grant Programs $50,000 to $200,000 is also a very important publication. It describes over 4,300 foundations that make annual grants of up to $200,000 but over $50,000.

Both *The Foundation Directory* and *The Foundation Directory, Part 2* are indexed according to the following:

- *Foundation Name* — If you know the name of a foundation that may be interested in elementary or middle school education, you can locate it in the Directories using this index. The index entry itself will provide you with one crucial piece of information — the state in which the foundation is registered. You need to know this to locate the foundation in the Directories, since the entries are in alphabetical order by state.

- *Subject Area* — Your Key Words Worksheet will provide you with the words you need to access this index and locate the foundations interested in your particular area. Elementary education is becoming increasingly popular as a subject of funding.

- *Types of Support* — Many foundations have severe restrictions on the types of funding they will support. This index enables you to quickly discover this important information.

- *Donor, Trustees, and Officers* — This index provides information that may help you develop linkages with foundations.

- *Geographic* — Foundations are listed under the state in which they are located. Foundations in boldface type make grants on a national, regional, or international basis. The others generally limit giving to the city or state in which they are located.

All of the indexes refer to the foundations by a four-digit number that appears above the foundation's name. As already mentioned, the foundations are arranged in alphabetical order according to the state in which they are incorporated. The first foundation listed in the fifteenth edition of *The Foundation Directory* is #1 Abroms Charitable Foundation, Inc., located in Alabama. The last is #6335 Wiancko Charitable Foundation, Inc., located in Wyoming.

The following fictitious entry is presented as it would be in *The Foundation Directory.*

Sample Entry
The Foundation Directory

2762
The Jessica Vastell Foundation
1651 North Broadway
Chicago 60604   (312) 896-9700

Incorporated in 1926 in IL.
Donor(s): Sabastian Vastell, Mrs. Jessica Vastell
Foundation type: Independent
Financial data (yr. ended 6/30/92): Assets, $150,444,176 (M); expenditures, $6,488,200, including $4,488,200 for 126 grants (high: $300,000; low: $200; average: $10,000-$50,000), $85,200 for 65 employee matching gifts and $1,200,200 for 7 foundation-administered programs.
Purpose and activities: Dedicated to enhancing the humane dimensions of life through activities that emphasize the theme of improving the quality of teaching and learning. Serves precollegiate education through grant making and program

activities in elementary and secondary public education.

Fields of interest: Elementary and secondary public education, teaching, social services, child welfare.

Types of support: Consulting services, technical assistance, special projects.

Limitations: No support for colleges and universities (except for projects in elementary and secondary education). No grants to individuals, or for building or endowment funds, or operating budgets; no loans.

Publications: Annual report, informational brochure (including application guidelines), financial statement, grants list.

Application information: Grant proposals for higher education not accepted; fellowship applications available only through participating universities. Application form not required.

    Initial approach: letter
    Copies of proposal: 1
    Deadline(s): None
    Board meeting date(s): May and Nov. and as required
    Final notification: 4 weeks
    Write: Dr. Andrew Brown, Pres.

Officers: Sabastian Vastell, Chair; Jessica Vastell, Vice-Chair. and Secy.; Andrew Brown, Pres.; Winifred L. Bower, V.P.; Franz Kirshbaumer, Treas.; Bilal Ali, Prog. Dir.

Trustees: John R. Lige, Virginia S. Smith, Donald C. Crowne, Jr., Charles Ludwig, George L. Sloan, P. John Cassidy.

Number of staff: 4 full-time professionals; 1 part-time professional; 4 full-time support.

Employer Identification Number: 679014579

In an effort to find a funder for our example project involving parent, teacher, and student involvement in responsible education, we turned to our key words and the subject index in *The Foundation Directory*. Using this resource, we were able to determine that the fictitious Jessica Vastell Foundation has expressed interest in elementary education. From the entry we were also able to ascertain that our request will fall within the foundation's average grant size of $10,000 to $50,000. However, we are still not ready to write a proposal to them or even to telephone them.

We need to learn more about the Jessica Vastell Foundation. For example, what do they *really* value? What types of projects have they funded? And to what types of organizations did they make their awards? Since *The Foundation Directory* entry does not state that the foundation limits its giving to any one geographic area, we are also interested in knowing where they have awarded their past grants.

Another popular Foundation Center publication, *The Foundation Grants Index*, can provide us with much of this information. *The Foundation Grants Index*, published annually, lists more than 58,000 grants made by 840 of the largest 33,000 foundations. The twenty-first edition (1993) indexes grant awards of $10,000 and larger. *The Foundation Grants Index* is divided into seven sections: 1. Grants Listing; 2. Grant Recipients; 3. Subject; 4. Type of Support/Geographic; 5. Recipient Category Index; 6. Index to Grants by Foundation; and 7. Foundation. Since we know the Vastell Foundation is in Illinois and have the foundation name, the following list of their grants can be easily located.

The following is a fictitious example of an entry in Section I of *The Foundation Grants Index*.

Sample Entry — Section I
The Foundation Grants Index
Education, Elementary and Secondary
Illinois

Vastell Foundation, Jessica, The

2713. Association of Indiana School Administrators, South Bend, IN. $28,000, 1992. For reorganization of schools project. 9/14/92.

2714. Association of Michigan School Administrators, Detroit, MI. $10,000, 1992. For Consortium for Schools of the Future. 10/21/92.

2715. Association of California School Administrators, Fresno, CA. $10,000, 1992. For reorganization of schools project. 10/10/91.

2716. Hazelnut School District, Hazelnut, MO. $11,000, 1992. For individualized alternative program for at-risk students. 6/9/92.

2717. Kids in Between, Kansas City, MO. $15,000, 1992. For educational program for teachers working with children of divorce. 10/15/92.

2718. Platterton School District, Agnes Middle School, Alexandria, VA. $13,000, 1992. For staff development activities related to Marginal Learners/Responsive School Project. 7/15/92.

From this list, we can see that the Jessica Vastell Foundation appears to exhibit values commensurate with our project. It appears that a grant of $25,000 would be reaching the Foundation's upper limit and that a proposal for $10,000 to $15,000 might stand a better chance for funding. Chapter 8 will provide you with more strategies for continuing your Values Approach to Grantseeking.

Besides having many excellent books on foundation funding, your Foundation Center Regional Library has two other references you should be familiar with.

- **The 990 Internal Revenue Service Foundation Tax Returns** — The Internal Revenue Service requires private foundations to file income tax returns each year. The 990-PF returns provide fiscal details on receipts and expenditures, compensation of officers, capital gains or losses, and other financial matters. Form 990-AR provides information on foundation managers, assets, and grants paid and/or committed for future payment. The Foundation Center's National Collections in New York City, San Francisco, Washington, D.C., and Cleveland have on microfiche the past three years of tax returns for all private foundations. Each Cooperating Collection has returns for private foundations located in its state and sometimes in surrounding states.

- **Grant Guides** — Published by the Foundation Center, these computer-produced guides to foundation giving are available in thirty subject areas. Each guide has three indexes — subject, geographic, and recipient.

Corporate Research Tools

The current federal IRS rules allow a corporation to take up to 10 percent of their gross profits as a tax deduction when these profits are given as grants to nonprofit organizations

(501(c)(3)s). However, I don't know of any corporations that give 10 percent. The national average is approximately 2 percent of gross profits.

In addition, not all corporate support is reflected in their tax deductible gifts. For example, when a corporation perceives that a potential grant project is blatantly self-serving (i.e., enhances marketplace positioning, product testing, or product development), they will often make the grant through their marketing department. This grant usually will not appear as a write-off against their taxable profits and will not show up on any grant list. This inability to verify corporate support accounts for the inaccuracy and lack of specificity that characterize the corporate grants marketplace.

What motivates a corporation to make a grant? What benefits can they receive by funding you? Reviewing the values of corporate funders tells us that they are motivated by a concern for:

- their workers and the children of their workers,
- product development, and
- product positioning.

In the example project to increase responsible educational behavior in parents, students, and teachers, the method or solution calls for the possible use of videotaping to provide a link between parent and teacher and between the student's level of performance and responsible educational practices. Companies in the area that have employees whose children attend the school may be interested in the project; and companies that make, sell, or distribute video recorders, players, and tapes may be interested even if they are outside the area. If the model project resulted in educational change, such companies would benefit, because in addition to the benefits related directly to education, a video equipment producer would also have the opportunity to position its products with parents and students — *future* consumers.

There are many reasons why companies support grant projects. But remember, they are not simply interested in doing nice things for education and for you. They want and expect a return on their investment.

How can you locate the companies that will be most interested in your project and its potential benefits? Your public library or local college library should have several helpful resources. In addition, if you are near a Foundation Center national collection or a regional cooperating collection, you have access to many resources, including two of the Foundation Center's primary corporate research tools — *The National Directory of Corporate Giving* and *Corporate Foundation Profiles.*

- ***The National Directory of Corporate Giving*** — This directory provides information on over 1,500 corporate foundations and on an additional 600 direct corporate-giving programs. It also has an extensive bibliography and six indexes to help you target funding prospects.
- ***Corporate Foundation Profiles*** — This publication contains detailed analyses of 247 of the largest corporate foundations in the United States. An appendix lists financial data on hundreds of additional corporations with assets of $1 million or a granting history of over $100,000 annually.

Since companies define themselves in terms of markets and products, it would help you to look at those funding prospects that might value your project because of its potential impact on their marketplace. *The Standard Industrial Classification Code Book,* available at your public library, is an excellent tool for finding out who makes what products. Once you have the names of the companies that manufacture the product you are interested in, you can telephone their local sales representatives or phone or write their corporate offices to find out their interest in your project.

One crucial fact to remember is that corporate grants decrease as profits go down. A look at *Dun and Bradstreet's Million Dollar Directory* will tell you the financial condition of 160,000 of America's largest businesses. If a company is paying its creditors late and owes money, it is *not* a prime target for a grant request.

OBTAINING CORPORATE GRANTS FROM COMPANIES IN YOUR COMMUNITY

Corporations in your area are your best bet for grant support. Start with companies near your school, where the children of the workers are served.

While corporations give where they live, they also expect a professional approach. Many companies require that their employees be volunteers or members of the nonprofit organization's advisory group before they will award it grant support. And just as companies are judged by the quality of their sales representatives, your school will be judged by the quality of the individual chosen to approach the company. I recommend that you always check with a district administrator before you contact a company. You can get a grant. Many elementary and middle school teachers have personally taken their proposals to corporations and have been quite successful.

Chambers of Commerce usually print an annual listing of all the companies in their area. The listing rank orders the companies by number of employees and payroll and often includes product information. This listing is an excellent grants research tool. Establish a Corporate Grants Advisory Group and invite several individuals from the corporate world to participate. One of them should be able to procure this invaluable list for you.

Since most corporations' grant money comes from their profits, knowing which local companies are profitable will be a big help. If you have a stockbroker on your Corporate Grants Advisory Group, ask the broker to find out which companies in your area are paying a stock dividend. In addition, companies are always concerned about their customers' credit ratings. How companies pay their bills is a reflection of their fiscal condition and profitability. Hence, companies subscribe to several services that help them keep close tabs on their customers. Ask the members of your Corporate Grants Advisory Group what services they use and if they could get you a report on the companies/corporations you are planning to approach.

Do not overlook smaller companies and independently owned businesses in your area. While individual companies or businesses may not be able to fund a grant idea on their own, several could band together to fund a project. Just because a company or business does not employ hundreds of individuals does not mean that it is not concerned about quality education. Like larger companies, smaller ones will expect to see a sound business plan as part of your proposal (more on this in chapter 10).

Other Research Tools

This chapter has given you information on materials that will help you in grantseeking.

Many of these materials are inexpensive or can be used free. The bibliography notes even more resources. In addition to the tools already mentioned, you may be interested in the many newsletters in the education/grants field. The following are those that I use in my work. I suggest that you contact the publishers for a free sample and subscription information.

- *Education Daily* — Capitol Publications, Inc., 1101 King Street, P.O. Box 1453, Alexandria, VA 22313–2053, 1–800–327–7203
- *Education Funding News* — Government Information Services, 1611 No. Kent Street, Suite 508, Arlington, VA 22209, 703–528–1082
- *Education Grants Alert* — Capitol Publications, Inc., 1101 King Street, P.O. Box 1453, Alexandria, VA 22313–2053, 1–800–327–7203
- *Federal Grants and Contracts Weekly* — Capitol Publications, Inc., 1101 King Street, P.O. Box 1453, Alexandria, VA 22313–2053, 1–800–327–7203
- *Foundation and Corporate Grants Alert* — Capitol Publications, Inc., 1101 King Street, P.O. Box 1453, Alexandria, VA 22313–2053, 1–800–327–7203
- *LRCW Newsbriefs* — Lutheran Resources Commission, Woodward Bldg., Suite 900, 733 15th St. NW, Washington, D.C. 20005, 202–667–9844

Ready — Aim — Go to chapter 8 to learn the basics on how to contact a grantor *before* you write your proposal.

CHAPTER EIGHT

Contacting the Grantor before You Write Your Proposal

This chapter may be the most important one in the entire book. If you are thinking of skipping it, think again. It is estimated that contacting the grantor before you write your proposal increases your chances of success between 300 and 500 percent! Preproposal contact results in grants success because it allows you to gather the information you need to view your project through the values glasses of the potential funder. *Nothing,* except getting funded, is better than face-to-face contact with a grantor. In-person contact allows you to discuss with the funder several possible approaches to the problem and to ascertain the grantor's interest in your solutions.

I know what you're thinking now. You're thinking, Wait a minute! Writing a proposal is one thing, but making preproposal contact with a prospective grantor is more than can be expected from a full-time teacher. I hear you! *But* you need to know how dramatically preproposal contact can affect the outcome. Besides, you need not be the individual who makes the contact. In fact, the best individual to make contact may be a volunteer. If you mobilized your grants effort through a grants advisory group, you may already have a volunteer with a sales and marketing background who would love to assist you. Contacting a funder will not cause a trained salesperson any anxiety. Remember, what is anxiety-producing for one person may not be for another. For example, your volunteer might find that facing your students for one day would be much more stressful than meeting face to face with a potential funding source.

Why Most Grantseekers Avoid Preproposal Contact

I ask many grantseekers why they avoid preproposal contact. While their answers vary, there is one consistent theme. Most individuals do not want to risk having their ideas rejected in a face-to-face meeting with a prospective grantor.

Whatever your reasons for avoiding preproposal contact, you must put them aside. Review your lists of connections and linkages for names of individuals who might be able to arrange preproposal contact with foundation or corporate board members, trustees, government bureaucrats, and so on. And remember, preproposal contact is not scary when you have done your "grants homework" and know enough about the prospective grantor to ask questions that reflect your knowledge rather than expose your ignorance.

Contacting Grantors

First, review the Grantseekers' Decision Matrix to remind yourself of the values and interests of the *type* of funder you have decided to approach. Then review the research you have collected on each *specific* grantor. Naturally, any procedural requirements of a particular funding source should be followed. In general, however, you will find the following suggestions helpful.

How to Contact Foundation and Corporate Grantors

SENDING FOR INFORMATION AND GUIDELINES

Many of the large foundations and corporations will mail you general information concerning their grants program including: grant application guidelines, annual reports, and newsletters. Use the Sample Letter to a Foundation/Corporation Requesting Information and Guidelines in figure 8.1 as a guide for contacting *only* those that have stated, as found in in your research, that application guidelines or other information is available. Those foundations and corporations that provide guidelines usually have a director and a staff to respond to your request.

Please note that this is an inquiry letter for information only. It is *not* a proposal to the foundation/corporation. Send this inquiry letter first, and if you get no response, you are justified in telephoning the foundation.

TELEPHONING FOUNDATIONS/CORPORATIONS

Fewer than 1,000 of the 33,000 foundations have offices. Therefore, telephone contact is

Figure 8.1

SAMPLE LETTER TO A FOUNDATION/CORPORATION
REQUESTING INFORMATION AND GUIDELINES

Date

Name
Title
Address

Dear [Contact Person]:

My research on your [foundation/corporation] indicates that you provide application guidelines to prospective grantees. I am developing a proposal in the area of [topic] and I would appreciate receiving these guidelines at your earliest convenience.

I would also appreciate any other information you may have that could help us prepare a successful, quality proposal. Please add us to your mailing list for annual reports, newsletters, priority statements, program statements, and so on.

Since both of our organizations are committed to [subject area] I believe you will find our proposal idea of interest. [Mention any linkage or volunteer support relative to the foundation's or corporation's employees. Also, the linkage could jointly sign the letter or send it themselves.]

Sincerely,

Name/Title
Phone Number

limited. Many of the entries in foundation resource directories do not list telephone numbers. Even if a phone number is listed in an entry or on an IRS tax return, *do not* call the foundation if the information clearly states that there should be *no contact except by letter.*

Corporations have more staff than foundations but value their time highly and allocate it to making money—not giving it away. With the larger grantors it is proper to send a letter first. Then telephone if you do not get a response.

In general, if you have a phone number for a foundation or corporation and you are not aware of any rules or instructions that discourage phone contact, you *should* telephone them. Of course, the optimum approach is to arrange a personal visit. If a face-to-face meeting is not possible, try to gather the same information you would in a visit via the telephone.

Fax it! The 1990s have added a new dimension to preproposal contact. When you talk to the foundation or corporate official to discuss your approaches to solving the problem, ask if you can fax her or him a one-page summary of your ideas, and call back to discuss the ideas. Try to arrange a mutually agreeable time to talk.

Steps for Contacting Foundation /Corporate Grantors

1. If appropriate, phone the contact person. Your purpose for calling is to validate the information you have already collected. Your questions should reflect your knowledge concerning the foundation's or corporation's granting pattern and priorities and elicit their interest in your approaches to solving a problem or increasing educational opportunities for elementary and middle school students. Introduce yourself and state the purpose of the call. (You may find it helpful to review your needs data before calling.) Remember, you are not calling for *yourself.* You're calling for your students, your school, and the field of education.

2. If you reach a secretary or administrative assistant, ask to talk to the foundation director, corporate contributions officer *or* to the staff person best able to answer your questions.

3. Demonstrate that you are different from other grantseekers. Show that you purposefully have *selected* their foundation/corporation by asking a question that reflects your research. For example, "I am contacting the ____________ Foundation/Corporation because you have demonstrated a desire to ____________. My research shows that 40 percent of your funds in recent years were committed to this area."

4. **Tell them what you want.** Example — "I would appreciate five minutes of your time to ascertain which of the approaches I have developed for the XYZ School would appeal to your board and elicit your foundation's greatest support." Note: You may use the fax approach here to maintain their interest.

   Remember, you are presenting the funder with an opportunity to meet *their needs.* You are not begging. They are looking for good programs to support. So get them excited about your project!

5. **My place or yours?** Your first choice is to *meet* with the funder. You would love to visit them to discuss your grant approaches. You would be happy to go to them, or they may be interested in coming to visit you at your school. By visiting you, they could observe

your students and see the needs population or problem firsthand. You would be happy *either* way. The funder will expect to pay their way to visit you and will expect you to pay your way to visit them.

6. **Who should be your representative(s)?** Whether you visit the funder or they come to you, your team should be small, usually no larger than two. Select an active and concerned volunteer from your grants advisory group who is *donating* her or his time to your proposed project/solution. The other person may be yourself or another paid professional.

7. **What should the team wear?** The rule of thumb is to dress the way the foundation official dresses. Although many individuals from the world of education are offended by the notion that people are judged by how they dress, it is worthwhile to take a look at *Dress for Success* by John T. Malloy. You may be surprised to learn that Malloy's original work was funded by a grant. His project was designed to test whether a classroom leader's way of dressing had an impact on students' learning and retention. The results of his research are quite interesting. Malloy found that the way a classroom teacher dresses does impact students' learning outcomes. While very few educators ever read the research findings or improved their dress habits because of them, corporations picked up on Malloy's findings. In short, you are judged by what you wear, so dress accordingly. Your project and students are worth your best effort to project a good image to the prospective funding source. But don't go overboard. Wear clothes you are comfortable in.

8. **What should the representative(s) take to the meeting?** What you take with you is extremely important. Focus on your objective. What do you expect to accomplish in a person-to-person visit with the potential grantor? You want:
   - agreement on the need or problem to be addressed,
   - a discussion of the prospective funder's interest in your proposed solution,
   - information on the grants decision process so you can tailor your approach, and
   - validation of your research and estimate on the amount of your grant request.

Avoid the common mistake of jumping directly to the money issue by concentrating on bringing material that solidifies agreement on the need or the problem. In many cases, the grantor has difficulty *seeing* what the problem looks like through the eyes of a student or an educator. Use the following techniques to help the funder develop insight into the problem. Your materials should be aimed at educating the grantor, not convincing them.

Videotapes — Make a short (three to five minutes) videotape that demonstrates the problem. A student-made tape can be very moving. Elementary and junior high students can make a short video as a class or school project. Whether it deals with alcohol abuse or zoology, a short video tells a compelling story because it enables the funder to *see* what the need is.

Slides and Audiotapes — As an example, I once had my students develop a five-minute slide presentation on alcohol use and abuse as a basis for a parent-child prevention program. We did not even have a machine that changed the slides automatically. We simply made an audiotape that played on a battery-operated cassette player that was started at the same time as the slide projector, set on three-second delay. The narrator was a volunteer from my Parent Advisory Group, who just happened to be a former radio announcer. Needless to say, the grantor was very impressed that this professional-looking and-sounding program was done by students and volunteers at a cost of less than $10!

Picture Book — A picture book that documents the need may provide the starting point for a discussion of how the funder views the problem.

Again, the objective of the meeting is to establish agreement on the need for a project and then to ascertain the funding source's interests and to discuss several approaches or solutions to the problem.

RECORDING YOUR RESEARCH AND PREPROPOSAL CONTACT

One reason for preproposal contact is to validate your research on the funding source and to add to that body of knowledge so that you can develop a grant-winning strategy. You want your research to be organized and to take advantage of every possible time-saving technique.

If you haven't already done so, establish a file for each of the grantors you are thinking about approaching. Keep the files together in alphabetical order. This will be a great start in organizing your grants effort.

Generate Foundation/Corporate Research Worksheets (fig. 8.2) for the grantors you believe are your most likely prospects for funding, based on your research. Use each worksheet to keep a record of the information you have gathered to date. Update the worksheet as you obtain additional information and materials. Also use the worksheet to log all contact made with the foundation/corporation, including face-to-face, telephone, and written contact.

In addition to information on a particular foundation, it is also important to collect as much information as you can on individual foundation officers, board members, and trustees. This information can help you determine ways to deal with any preferences and biases you may encounter and to locate other possible linkages between the foundation, your school, a volunteer on your Grants Advisory Group, and so on.

Use the Foundation/Corporate Funding Staff History Worksheet (fig. 8.3) to record the information you collect. Store the worksheet in the appropriate foundation's file.

Steps for Contacting Government Grantors

1. Contact with government agencies is encouraged by letter, phone, and, when possible, in person. The first step is to send the agency a letter requesting program information and to be put on the agency's mailing list. Use the Sample Letter to a Federal Agency Requesting Information and Guidelines (fig. 8.4) when appropriate.

2. Next, telephone the federal agency that you have discovered in your search. *The Catalogue of Federal Domestic Assistance* may provide you with an individual's name as well as with the agency's phone number. Have at hand the name of the informational contact you developed from your research, but don't be surprised if the person listed in your research has moved on or is not the best individual to assist you.

Figure 8.2

Foundation/Corporation: _______________________ **Deadline Date(s):** ___________

Foundation/Corporation Research Worksheet

Create a file for each private grantor you are researching and place all the information in this file. Use this research worksheet to:

* keep a record of the information you have gathered
* maintain a log of all telephone and face-to-face contact with the foundation
* log all correspondence sent to and received from the grantor

---

Address: Name of Contact Person:

Telephone Number: Title of Contact Person:

Fax Number:

Place a check mark (√) next to the information you have gathered and placed in the file for the foundation.

______ Description of the granting program

  Note Source: ____

______ Information on past grants

  Note Source: ____

______ Application Information/Guidelines

  ______ Sent for   ______ Received

______ Annual Report

  ______ Sent for   ______ Received

______ Newsletter/Other Reports

  ______ Sent for   ______ Received

______ Funding Staff History

______ Written Summary of Each Contact Made

______ Grantor Strategy Worksheet

______ List of Board Members/Officers

______ 990 IRS Tax Return (Foundations Only)

______ Financial/Profit Statements (Corporations Only)

______ Chamber of Commerce Data (Corporations only)

______ Product Information/SIC Code (Corporations Only)

Record of Face-to-Face and Telephone Contact:

Date Contacted	Contacted by	Foundation Contact	Results	Action

Record of All Correspondence Sent and Received:

Date of Correspondence	Purpose of Correspondence	Results/Action

Figure 8.3

Foundation/Corporation: ____

FOUNDATION/CORPORATE FUNDING STAFF HISTORY WORKSHEET

1. Name of Director/Contributions Officer: _______________________________

2. Title: ____

3. Residence Address: ___________________________ Phone _________________

4. Business Telephone: ___________________________ Phone _________________

5. Linkages/Contacts (Mutual Friends/Associates who can contact Director/Contributions Officer
   for you): ____

   ____

   ____

   List any data you have uncovered that might help you:
   • determine ways to deal with any of contact's preferences and biases
   • locate other possible linkages between this individual and you/your school/a
     volunteer on your Grants Advisory Group, etc.

6. Birthdate: ____________________ Birthplace: __________________________

7. Marital Status: _______________ Children: ___________________________

8. Employer: ____________________ Job Title: __________________________

9. College/University: ___________________ Degree(s) __________________

10. Military Service: ____

11. Clubs/Affiliations: ____

12. Interests/Hobbies: ____

13. Other Board Memberships: ____

14. Other Philanthropic Activities: ______________________________________

15. Awards/Honors: ____

16. Other: ____

Notes:

SAMPLE LETTER TO A FEDERAL AGENCY REQUESTING
INFORMATION AND GUIDELINES

Date

Name
Title
Address
Dear [Contact Person]:

I am interested in the grant opportunities under [C.F.D.A. #], [Program Title]. Please add my name to your mailing list to receive information on this program. I am particularly interested in receiving application forms, program guidelines, and any existing priorities statements.

Please also send any other information that could help me prepare a quality application, such as a list of last year's successful grant recipients and reviewers. I am enclosing a self-addressed envelope for your convenience in sending these lists.

I will be contacting you when it is appropriate to discuss my proposal ideas. Thank you for your assistance.

Sincerely,

Name/Title
Phone Number

Inform the person who answers the phone that you are calling for information concerning one of their grant programs and tell them the CFDA reference number and the name of the granting program.

3. It usually takes one or two referrals to get the correct person and program. Introduce yourself and ask to speak with the program officer or with someone who can answer a few brief but important questions.

4. Demonstrate your knowledge, *not* your ignorance. Your research has provided you with a considerable amount of information. Use this opportunity to validate it. Check the accuracy of the deadline dates and appropriations printed in the CFDA.

5. **Tell them what you want!** Ask for a few minutes of their time. These are employees of your federal (or state) government. Remember, there is more support staff involved in the government grants process than the foundation or corporate, and Freedom of Information rules must be observed in tax-supported grantseeking. Staff members are generally helpful and willing, if not eager, to provide information.

Your objective is to discuss your approaches to solving the problem. Some federal programs actually request a preproposal meeting or submission of a concept paper. Believe it or not, they want you to submit the best possible proposal, even if they are unable to fund it. The better your proposal and the more requests they receive, the more their program is needed.

Your first choice is to visit the federal agency in Washington, D.C. If you cannot, and you do not have a volunteer who can make a visit for you, a phone conversation is your best alternative. Again, ask permission to fax them a one-page concept paper and to call after they have had time to review it. Ask the contact person to place you on the agency's mailing list to receive guidelines, application information, newsletters, and so on.

Review the diagram of the Proactive Grantseekers' $75 Billion Federal Grants Clock in figure 8.5 and ask where the agency is in the grants process.

Federal Register — Have they published anything in *The Federal Register* on their rules? If so, ask for the date of publication and the page number.

Past Grantees — Request a list of last year's grantees. The list will tell you *who* got *how much* grant money and will help you determine if your school/community stands a chance of receiving funds or if you would be better off developing a consortium with other districts, joining with your intermediate district, or becoming part of a college or university's grant.

Figure 8.5

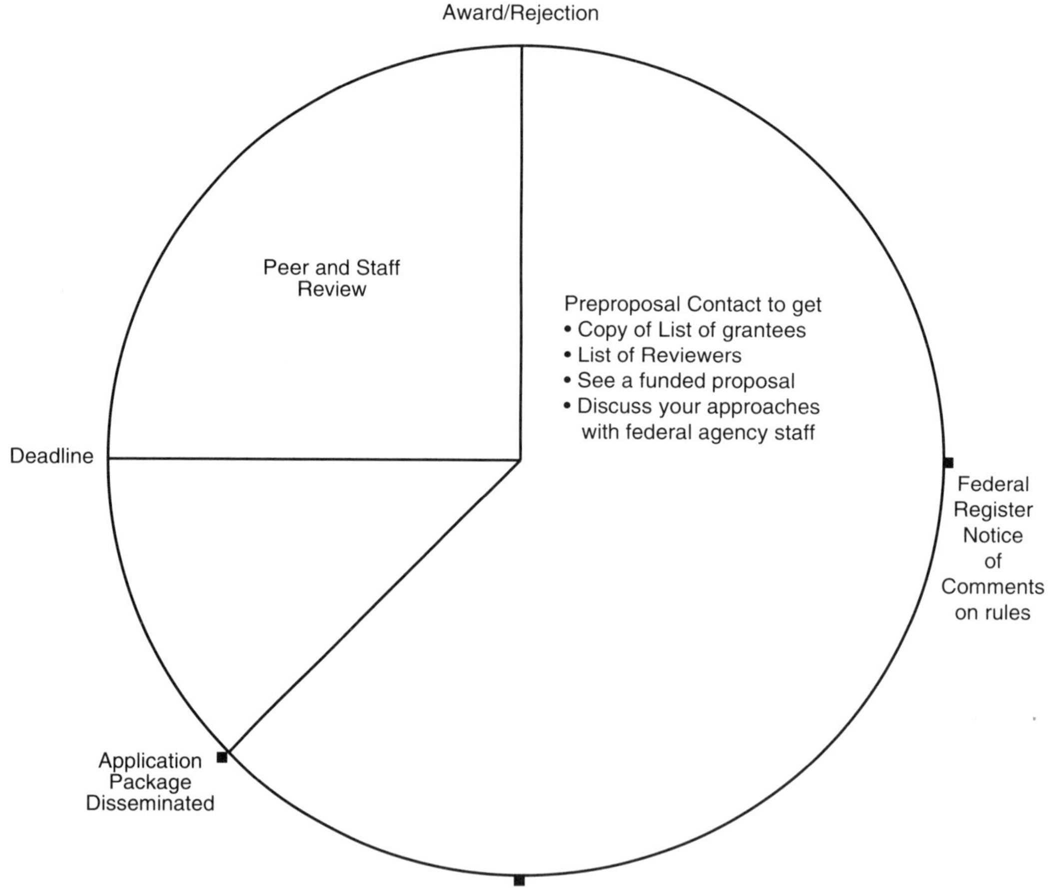

THE PROACTIVE GRANTSEEKERS' $75 BILLION FEDERAL GRANTS CLOCK

The clock operates 365 days a year. The federal government's year begins on October 1 and ends September 30.

Past Reviewers — Ask the agency official for information on the agency's peer review system. While *The Federal Register* may have information on the points that the reviewers award for each section of a proposal, you need to know who reads the grant applications. Request a list of last year's reviewers. Knowing the types of reviewers and their backgrounds will help you determine what writing style to use and how to construct your proposal.

In addition, you should ask the program officer how you could become a reviewer so you can learn more about the review process.

6. **My place or yours?** You would like to meet in Washington, D.C., or at a federal regional office, if one exists. You could also invite the funding official to visit your school to observe the problem firsthand. She or he may come if you invite other schools and districts to attend an informative session on grants available through that agency.

   You may also ask the program officer what educational conferences or professional meetings she or he is planning to attend in the near future. You may be able to meet with the official at a meeting near your school.

7. **Who should represent you at the meeting?** You could send a volunteer from your grants advisory group. Of course, the best approach would be for you to go with the volunteer. Two is the magic number when it comes to representation. If you send more than two, the federal program officer will begin to wonder who is back home teaching!

8. **What should the representative(s) wear?** Federal program officers are usually quite conservative. But there is a difference in dress between the Department of Education and the National Endowment for the Humanities. Program officers usually dress more casually in the arts and humanities than in education and science. Dress as much like the program officer as possible. The older the bureaucrat, the more conservative the dress. Malloy's book *Dress for Success* has a section on how to dress for meetings with government bureaucrats.

9. **What should the representative(s) take to the meeting?** Take materials that help demonstrate the need. These may include audiovisual aids such as short (three to five minutes) filmstrips, videotapes, slide presentations, pictures, and so on. In addition, representatives may leave with the official information on your community, school district, school, or classroom. But *never* leave a proposal.

   Your representatives may also want to have with them, or better yet, commit to memory, a list of questions to ask the program officer.

RECORDING FEDERAL RESEARCH AND PREPROPOSAL CONTACT

Keep copies of the information you gather on a prospective government funding source and record all contacts and correspondence on the Federal Research Worksheet in figure 8.6. Record all information you gather on agency personnel on the Federal Funding Staff History Worksheet (fig. 8.7).

The Grantor Strategy Worksheet

Complete a Grantor Strategy Worksheet (fig. 8.8) for each funding source you plan to

CFDA No. _________________________________ **Deadline Date(s):** _____________

Program Title: _______________________________ **Gov't. Agency:** _____________

Federal Research Worksheet

Create a file for each program you are researching and place all the information you gather on this program in the file. Use this Federal Research Worksheet to:

* keep a record of the information you have gathered
* maintain a log of all telephone and face-to-face contacts made with the government agency
* log all correspondence sent to and received from the agency

Agency Address: Agency Director:

Telephone Number: Program Director:

Fax Number: Name/Title of Contact Person:

Place a check mark (√) next to the information you have gathered and placed in the file for the foundation.

_______ Program Description from CFDA

_______ Letter Requesting to be put on mailing list

    _______ Sent for   _______ Received

_______ List of last year's grantees

    _______ Sent for   _______ Received

_______ List of last year's reviewers

    _______ Sent for   _______ Received

_______ Application package — expected availability date

    _______ Sent for   _______ Received

_______ Comments on rules/final rules from *Federal Register*

_______ Notice of rules for evaluation from *Federal Register*

_______ Grant Scoring System — Point allocation for each section

    Source: ____

_______ Sample funded proposal

_______ Federal Funding Staff History Worksheet

_______ Written summary of each contact made

_______ Grantor Strategy Worksheet

Record of Face-to-Face and Telephone Contact:

Date Contacted	Contacted by	Foundation Contact	Results	Action

Record of All Correspondence Sent and Received:

Date of Correspondence	Purpose of Correspondence	Results/Action

CFDA No. ____

Program Title: ____

Gov't. Agency: ____

FEDERAL FUNDING STAFF HISTORY WORKSHEET

1. Name: ____

2. Title: ____
    (Agency Director, Program Director, Program Officer, etc.)

3. Business Address: _______________________________________

4. Business Telephone: _____________________________________

5. Birthdate: _________________________ Birthplace: _______________________

6. Marital Status: _________________________ Children: _______________________

7. College/University: _______________________________________

8. Degree(s): ____

9. Military Service: ____

10. Clubs/Affiliations: _______________________________________

11. Interests/Hobbies: _______________________________________

12. Board Memberships: _______________________________________

13. Other Philanthropic Activities: ___________________________

14. Awards/Honors: ____

15. Other: ____

Notes:

submit a proposal to. This worksheet will help you develop a tailored approach to each funding source. It will also help you understand the funder's point of view.

Take full advantage of your ability to analyze the funding source's granting history. Even if you have not been able to make preproposal contact, it is imperative that the amount you are requesting fits the funding source's granting pattern.

Think about whom you might collaborate with on your proposal and what group might better serve as the submitting organization.

Make every attempt to find out *who* will be reading and evaluating your proposal. For example, will your proposal be read by staff members? board members? program personnel? outside experts/reviewers? This information not only will help you write your proposal; it is also vital to performing a mock review, which will be discussed in chapter 12.

Rank order the funding sources that represent your best prospects. Eventually, you will tailor your proposal to those at the top of the list.

You probably will be missing some vital pieces of information. But based on what you have, devise the best strategy you can, and go for it!

Once you have determined your strategy, go on to chapter 9 to learn how to develop objectives.

Potential Grantor: _________________________________ **Priority #:** _________________

Deadline: ____

GRANTOR STRATEGY WORKSHEET

A. Strategy Derived from Granting Pattern
1. $______ Largest Grant to Organization Most Similar to Ours
2. $______ Smallest Grant to Organization Most Similar to Ours
3. $______ Average Grant Size to Organizations Similar to Ours
4. $______ Average Grant Size in Our Area of Interest
5. $______ Our Estimated Grant Request
6. Financial Trend in Our Area of Interest Over Past Three Years
   Up ___________ Down ___________ Stable ___________
7. If your proposal is a multiyear proposal, how popular have these been with the funding source in the past three years?
   _______ Many Multiyear Proposals Funded
   _______ Some Multiyear Proposals Funded
   _______ Few Multiyear Proposals Funded
   _______ No Multiyear Funding
   _______ Not Applicable
8. Financial Data on Funding Source: Obligation Levels for Last Three Years for Grants
   19 ______ $________ 19 ______ $________ 19 ______ $________

B. Based on preproposal contact, which solution strategies are the most appropriate for this funding source?

____

____

____

____

C. Proposal Review System
1. Who evaluates submitted proposals? _______________________________________

____

2. What is the background and training of the evaluators? ___________________

____

____

3. What point system will be followed? _______________________________________

____

____

____

4. How much time will be spent reviewing each proposal? ___________________

____

____

D. Use this space to note anything "special" that will affect proposal outcome.

____

____

CHAPTER NINE

Developing Objectives

Through preproposal contact, you will determine which of your solutions appeals most to the prospective grantor. This will help you decide which solution to propose. Once you have selected the best solution or approach, you must develop your proposal objectives. An objective is a measurable step taken to narrow or close the gap between what is and what ought to be. A well-constructed objective tells the funding source what will change as a result of the funds they provide.

Many grantseekers do not understand the difference between an objective and a method. Some actually write objectives that focus on the approaches or methods that will be utilized to bring about the change. This confuses *what* will be accomplished with *how* it will be accomplished.

To be sure you have developed a well-constructed objective, ask yourself if there is more than one way to reach your objective. If the objective you are testing suggests that there is only one possible approach, then you are dealing with a solution, not an objective. By asking yourself why you are performing a particular activity, you may back into your objective. In doing so, you will strengthen your proposal and develop a clear sense of *what* you will measure as you close the gap in the area of need.

An objective provides a measurable way to "see" how much change will occur by the conclusion of the project. A method tells *how* this change will be accomplished. A simple rule of thumb is:

Objectives tell what you want to accomplish, and methods tell how you will accomplish it.

Developing objectives may seem tedious, especially when you are eager to write your proposal. But keep in mind that well-written objectives that focus on the measurable change to be accomplished will make your proposal more interesting and compelling to the funder and will enable you to measure the changes the proposal suggests.

In addition, when writing a proposal, most grantseekers want to move quickly to *how* they will do their project instead of first presenting *what* is to be accomplished. Measurement and evaluation to these grantseekers often focus on such issues as *how many* students will be exposed to a new piece of equipment or teaching regime rather than *what* the students will be able to do as a result of the experience. Well-written objectives will help combat this problem.

While this primer outlines a process for developing well-constructed objectives, the ultimate judge of a "good" objective is the *grantor*. There are vast differences in the ways grantors prefer objectives to be written. By procuring a copy of a funded proposal and discussing your proposal idea with the funding source prior to submission, you will obtain a much more accurate idea of what they consider a "good" objective and therefore have a better chance of winning support.

If you are unable to obtain a funded proposal or make preproposal contact to discuss your approach, the Objectives Worksheet at the end of this chapter and the following guidelines for developing objectives will provide you with a secure basis for organizing your approach. In general, a "good" objective has the following components:

- an action verb and a statement,
- a measurement indicator,
- a performance standard,
- a deadline, and
- a cost frame.

1. Action Verb and Statement — What Will Change as a Result of the Successful Completion of Your Project

First review your Needs Worksheet and your Goals Worksheet. Remember, you are not suggesting or promising that the goal *will* be met and the gap *entirely* eliminated. You are *suggesting* that a measurable part of the gap will be closed through the grant and the successful completion of your prescribed actions. Do not worry because you are not *certain* that your proposed solution, model project, or research proposal will be 100 percent *successful*. You are *proposing* a solution, and even if it is unsuccessful, the field of education will learn from the experience.

For instance, in the example of the project to promote educationally responsible behavior in parents, teachers, and students, it is unlikely that the proposed approach will result in closing the gap *entirely*. But we can't measure what we can't state! Put simply, the project will *increase* educationally responsible behavior in parents, teachers, and students. However, this does not mean that it will *eradicate* irresponsible behavior.

As a professional educator, you probably studied how to construct behavioral objectives in college. You may now find it helpful to retrieve the appropriate texts from your bookshelf. For instance, *Taxonomy of Educational Objectives, Handbook I: The Cognitive Domain* will help you develop knowledge-centered objectives, and *Taxonomy of Educational Objectives, Handbook II: The Affective Domain* will help you develop values-centered objectives.

When you ask what will change as a result of your project, you may find that some of your answers fall in the realm of knowledge and others in the realm of values and feelings. In the example concerning educationally responsible behavior in students, teachers, and parents, some outcomes might be cognitive and others affective, which means that you would attempt to develop behavior that reflects both knowledge and appreciation of the value of education.

2. Measurement Indicator — How You Will Measure the Area You Are Attempting to Change

Just as there are many ways to accomplish your objectives, there are often several strategies that can measure the change in your area of need. Begin by asking what a student would do differently after you provided her or him with your solution or method of solving the problem.

Cognitive skills are usually the easiest to measure. In many cases, tests for this purpose already exist. For instance, there are standardized tests that can measure an increase in reading ability. If there is not a test available, you can always include the task of developing one in your proposal.

Literacy rates can be easily measured, as can computer literacy, math skills, and so on. But how do we measure values?

To determine how to measure values, feelings, and/or attitudes, ask yourself how an individual would act who already values the desired outcome. For example, if the desired outcome of a project is to instill an appreciation for Elizabethan literature, you would ask how a student who already values Elizabethan literature acts. You may decide that students who truly like Elizabethan literature read it for their own satisfaction and not just to fulfill an assignment. If this is the case, you could add a component to your project that calls for placing several works of Elizabethan literature in the school library and then keeping a record of their use.

If your project deals with performing arts, you might consider measuring appreciation by the number of students who attend a performance on their own, sign up for the school band, volunteer to work on the class play, and so on.

In one proposal I worked on, the objective was to increase teenagers' sense of responsibility toward alcohol consumption. Once the activities and methods were chosen, I was responsible for determining how the outcome would be measured. I decided that we would analyze certain pre- and postproject statistics, such as the number of alcohol-related deaths and accidents and of driving-while-intoxicated (DWI) charges. We would also administer a pre- and posttest to measure attitudinal changes concerning the subject. I developed a Responsible Drinking Scale and evaluated the responses to this survey in conjunction with statistics taken from police records.

In the project to increase educationally responsible behavior in parents, teachers, and students, we can measure the closing of the gap between what exists now and what ought to be in a variety of ways. For instance, we could look for behavior we believe is indicative of a developing sense of responsibility in the educational process, such as:

- improved grades
- decrease in absenteeism
- increase in the number of students who successfully complete their grades
- increase in time spent on homework
- increase in the number of teacher/parent contacts
- increase in parent/child discussions about education
- decrease in hours spent watching television

We might even develop an Educational Responsibility Scale that contains questions aimed at surveying many of the points outlined above.

3. Performance Standard — Amount of Change Necessary to Consider the Project Successful

A grantor will look at your objectives, make note of the amount you are requesting, examine your measurement indicators, and compare the amount of your request with the expected amount of change.

For example, if a project proposes to increase the reading scores of a certain target population from the 50th to the 70th percentile as measured by the Flockmeister Reading Scale, the percentile increase needs to be justified according to:

- the number and type of students in the target population,
- the cost per student, and
- the long-term effects of such an increase.

If the increase can be correlated to an increase in the likelihood of students graduating from grade school, junior high, and eventually high school and can be brought about at a cost of $100 per student rather than $1,000, the grantor is likely to think the percentile increase very meaningful.

In the sample project to increase responsible educational behavior in parents, students, and teachers, we might be able to show a percentage increase by developing a scale that would survey several of the behavioral indicators previously mentioned. Thus far the objective might look something like this:

> To increase the responsible educational behavior of parents, students, and teachers in the XYZ Elementary School [action verb and statement] by 25 percent [performance standard], as measured by the Responsible Education Scale [measurement indicator].

4. Deadline — Time Needed to Accomplish the Desired Degree of Change

When you are dealing with government grants this issue is usually decided for you. Most government grants are for one year. This is because of the way the budget appropriation cycle operates. However, there is currently a movement to allow multiyear awards because it is difficult to *create* the behavioral change outlined in an objective in just 12 months. In addition, it often takes a good part of 12 months just to develop and conduct a pretest that provides the baseline data for the posttest.

In dealing with a multiyear project, you may want to create your objective with a one-year goal for change and increase the change indicated in the measurement indicator over the subsequent years. For example, in the educationally responsible behavior project, the objective could indicate a 25 percent increase in year one and a 40 percent increase by the end of year two.

5. Cost Frame — How Much It Will Cost

Include the cost of accomplishing the change in the body of your objective. This provides a stark reminder of how much it costs to accomplish change. It also demonstrates that you have a total command of your proposal. You know "what it is" that will be accomplished, how much will be accomplished, and at what cost.

However, in most cases you cannot include cost in an objective until you have completed your budget. The Project Planner in Chapter 10 will help you develop a budget that shows you the cost of each objective. Once you have completed your Project Planner, go back to your objectives and add a cost component to each.

To determine the cost of developing change more accurately, divide the total cost of the project by the number of students it will serve. This will give you the cost per student served. If the cost per student served appears to be high, ask yourself how many students will benefit in *future* years and how many students at other schools will benefit once you disseminate your information to them. Proposals that contain equipment may seem excessively expensive, particularly when you think in terms of only one classroom. But when you take into consideration that the equipment will be utilized for five years and that it will be shared with other classrooms, the cost per student served will seem much more acceptable.

In the 1970s many demonstration models were developed that never could be replicated because the cost per person served was excessive. Funding sources are trying not to repeat this mistake. By keeping your eye on the cost of accomplishing your objectives and creating the change you desire, you can keep education grounded in economic reality.

OBJECTIVES WORKSHEET

Review your Needs and Goals Worksheets from chapter 4. This will help you develop objectives that take demonstrable steps to close the gap between what exists now and what should be. If you are able to study a copy of a funded proposal, take note of the way the objectives are constructed. Always defer to the grantor's guidelines and/or the example provided by successful proposals. When in doubt, or when lacking information, use the following format to help you construct winning objectives.

Format: To [action verb and statement] by [performance standard] as measured by [measurement indicator] by [time frame] at a cost of $[cost frame].

Example: To <u>increase completion rates</u> in Smith Elementary School by <u>50%</u>, as measured by the <u>Smith School Completion Rate</u>, <u>in one year</u>, at a cost of <u>$20,000</u>.

---

1. What is the area you expect to see change in as a result of the successful completion of your methods?
    (Example: completion rates)

2. How much change (performance standard) do you forecast as an index of your success?
    (Example: 50% increase in completion rates)

3. What measurement indicator will you use to denote the change?
    (Example: Smith School Completion Rate)

4. How long will it take to implement your proposal and measure the change?
    (Example: one year)

5. How much will it cost to accomplish your objective:
    (Example: $20,000)

CHAPTER TEN

Developing a Project Planner

Only after you have uncovered as much information about the prospective grantor as you can and completed a Grantor Strategy Worksheet should you begin to finalize your project design. In the ideal situation, you will have already presented the prospective grantor with several interesting alternatives and explored the grantor's interest in your project and the amount of investment they are ready to make. Many grantseekers make the mistake of writing their proposals first, before they look for grantors. Besides resulting in a limited number of potential grantors, this approach is usually unsuccessful because grantseekers are often reluctant to change their approaches or project designs to accommodate funders once they have written their proposals.

Even if you are unable to utilize the preproposal contact strategies previously outlined in this primer, you must choose the solution or approach that is most likely to offer the prospective grantor what they want. Your research should have at least uncovered the funder's range of grant awards. If your proposal requires more funds than a single grantor is likely to invest, you will need a project plan that specifies the funds you are requesting from each funder and shows what parts of your project each grantor will fund.

The Values-based Approach to Grantseeking requires that you view your proposal through the eyes of the funder and that you provide each prospective funder with a plan that is tailored to their needs. The funder may not see the methods, the budget, or the grant request the same way that you do, and each type of grantor will view these issues differently. For example, government grantors prefer well-organized proposals that allow them to easily identify matching or in-kind contributions and may require a budget narrative that links each expenditure to a method. Most corporate and foundation funders operate under an entirely different set of expectations. They often apply a business approach to their grant decision making and cost analysis.

Irrespective of the *type* of funding source, *all* grantors require that you have a plan. Just as you require student teachers to have a well-developed lesson plan before you give them access to your pupils and classroom, funding sources require grantees to have a well-developed plan before they give them access to their funds. The Project Planner ™ in figure 10.1 provides for this. The Project Planner is reprinted with permission from the American Council on Education.

Think of the Project Planner as your lesson plan. Write the plan when you have a good idea of the preferred solution, who your key staff will be, your consortium arrangements, and the matching or in-kind contributions you will have.

The Project Planner will help you:

- develop a clearly defined, proposal methodology, and
- conceptualize your grant plan and budget.

Once completed, the Project Planner will allow you to define and refine several aspects of your project, including:

1. An adequate staffing pattern that describes *who* is needed to do *what* tasks *when* (This will help ensure that your job descriptions match the tasks that need to be accomplished.)

2. An easily scanned overview of the prescribed activities and how they relate to cost and the attainment of the objectives

3. A logical framework in which to evaluate the tasks performed by consultants

4. A detailed analysis of the materials, supplies, and equipment related to each objective

5. A defensible budget and cash forecast

6. An efficient way to document your in-kind or matching component

The Project Planner will appeal most to those funding sources that are familiar with and use spreadsheet formats. The Project Planner is a particularly effective tool in government proposals. Today more than ever federal program officers push grantees to carry out their entire proposals as presented for amounts less than requested. Because federal budget forms use broad budget categories, it is difficult to negotiate final awards. Standard federal budget forms make it difficult to demonstrate to the funder how a specific objective will be impacted by a reduction in funds. By using the Project Planner, the grantee can show how a reduction in funds will mean a reduction in the specific methods or activities performed, which will affect the ability to achieve the proposal's objectives, which ultimately affects the ability to bring about the desired change. The Project Planner will allow you to present a clear picture of the relationship between project personnel, consultants, equipment and supplies, and the accomplishment of your proposal.

General Guidelines for Completing a Project Planner

1. Column A/B — Objectives and Methods

- List your project objectives and label each. For example, Objective A, Objective B, Objective C, and so on.

- List the methods you will use to accomplish each of the objectives. Think of the methods as the tasks or activities you will use to meet the need. Label each of the methods under its appropriate objective. For example, A - 1, B - 1, C - 1, and so on.

2. Column C/D — Month

- Record the month you will begin each activity or task and the month you will end each activity or task. For example, 1/4 would mean you intend to begin the first month after you receive funding and carry out the activities over 4 months (16 weeks). If you know the expected start-up month, you can use it.

3. Column E — Time

- Record the number of person hours, weeks, or months needed to accomplish each task listed in column A/B.

4. Column F — Project Personnel

- List the names of the key personnel who will spend a measurable or significant amount of time on each task or activity listed and on the accomplishment of each objective. (You have already recorded the time under column E.)

PROJECT PLANNER™

Sheet _______ of _______

Proposal Developed for ____

PROJECT TITLE: ____

PROJECT DIRECTOR: ____

Proposed starting date _______________   Proposal Year _______________

A. List Project objectives or outcomes A. B.
B. List Methods to accomplish each objective as A-1, A-2, A-3 . . . B-1, B-2 . . .

	MONTH		TIME	PROJECT PERSONNEL	PERSONNEL COSTS			CONSULTANTS • CONTRACT SERVICES			NON-PERSONNEL RESOURCES NEEDED SUPPLIES • EQUIPMENT • MATERIALS				SUB-TOTAL COST FOR ACTIVITY	MILESTONES PROGRESS INDICATORS	
	BEGIN	END			SALARIES & WAGES	FRINGE BENEFITS	TOTAL	TIME	COST/WEEK	TOTAL	ITEM	COST/ITEM	QUANTITY	TOT. COST	TOTAL I, L, P	ITEM	DATE
	C / D		E	F	G	H	I	J	K	L	M	N	O	P	Q	R	S

TOTAL DIRECT COSTS OR COSTS REQUESTED FROM FUNDER ▶

MATCHING FUNDS, IN-KIND CONTRIBUTIONS, OR DONATED COSTS ▶

TOTAL COSTS ▶

T   ◀ % OF TOTAL

◀

100%   ◀

5. Columns G/H/I — Personnel Costs

- Column G — Salaries & Wages
- Column H — Fringe Benefits
- Column I — Total

For each key person listed in column F you will need to provide an estimate of his or her salary/wage and fringe benefits. You can come up with a rough job description by listing the activities he or she will be responsible for and the minimum qualifications you require. You can determine whether he or she will be full- or part-time by looking at the number of hours, weeks, or months that person will be needed. Once you have developed a rough job description, you can call a placement agency to get an estimate of the salary needed to fill the position.

Be sure to analyze whose services from your organization will be *donated*. Put an asterisk next to all donated personnel and remember that their fringes as well as their wages will be donated. Identifying donated personnel is crucially important when the grantor requires matching or in-kind contributions. However, it may be advantageous to designate donated personnel even when matching contributions are not a requirement. Matching contributions show good faith and make you seem a better investment to the funding source. In fact, put an asterisk by *anything* you donate (e.g., supplies, equipment, materials) as you complete the remaining columns.

6. Columns J/K/L — Consultants/Contract Services

- Column J — Time
- Column K — Cost/Week
- Column L — Total

These three columns refer to individuals who are not in your normal employ and to services not normally provided by someone in your organization. (Note: No fringe benefits are paid to these individuals.)

7. Columns M/N/O/P Nonpersonnel Resources Needed: Supplies, Equipment, Materials

- Column M — Item
- Column N — Cost/Item
- Column O — Quantity
- Column P — Total Cost

Use these four columns to list the supplies, equipment, and materials needed to complete each activity and to itemize the associated costs. Do not underestimate the resources needed to achieve your objectives and successfully complete the project. Ask yourself and your key personnel what is needed to complete each activity. Again, designate donated items with an asterisk.

8. Column Q — Subtotal Cost for Activity

- Column Q is derived by adding together Columns I, L, and P — the total for personnel costs, consultant/contract services, and nonpersonnel resources. You can do this either for each individual activity or for each objective. If you do this for each objective, you will have to add together the subtotals for all of the activities falling under that objective.

9. Columns R/S — Milestones/Progress Indicators

- Column R — List what you will provide the funding source that tells them how you are working toward accomplishing your objectives (e.g., quarterly report). Think of these as milestones or progress indicators.
- Column S — Record the dates the funding source will receive the listed milestones or progress indicators.

There are many way to complete the Project Planner. The key is to make sure your Project Planner *works for you* as you plan and implement your proposal. It will help you develop a clear picture of the personnel, consultant services, equipment, and materials your project will require and of the relationship between these elements and your objectives. It should be thought of as a tool to help you take into account *all* the costs of completing the methods and activities in your plans and document the costs that will be borne by each partner in the agreement.

If you are not familiar with spreadsheets, the Project Planner can seem a bit overwhelming. But remember, the only *real* mistakes you can make when completing the Project Planner are mathematical ones (e.g., incorrect addition, multiplication, and so on). You control how detailed your Project Planner is. It should work for *you*.

Project Planner — Sample A

Project Planner — Sample A (fig. 10.2) provides you with some insight into *one* way the Project Planner can be completed.

In Sample A the project director's salary is being requested of the funder, as are the salaries of two graduate students who will be assisting the project director. The services of the project director and the graduate students are being contracted from West State University. Therefore, their time commitments and costs fall in columns J, K, and L (Consultants/Contract Services) on the Project Planner.

The project director, Dr. Smith, will have West State University's Human Subjects Institutional Review Board examine the procedures to get the student, parents, and teachers to agree to write contracts for change. It is anticipated that he will work on the project for 12 weeks …approximately half-time…during months 1 through 6, and 24 weeks (full-time) during months 7 through 12.

Sample A shows a considerable amount of matching/in-kind contributions, as indicated by the asterisks (*). For example, the school district is donating the salary and fringe benefits for the project secretary. In addition, a significant portion of the matching/in-kind contributions is coming from the Jones Corporation, which is donating the use of its corporate video production facility.

While matching and in-kind contributions demonstrate frugality, commitment, and hard work, "overmatching" can become an issue. When a proposal has a huge matching component and requires only a small amount of grant funds, a prospective grantor may get the impression that the *entire* proposal should be funded through matching and in-kind contributions. However, grantors view *most* matching components very favorably.

PROJECT PLANNER™

SAMPLE A

Sheet ____ of ____

Proposal Developed for ________________________

PROJECT TITLE: A Contract for Educational Cooperation – Parents, Teachers & Students Charting a Course for Involvement

PROJECT DIRECTOR: ________________________

Proposed starting date ____ Proposal Year ____

A. List Project objectives or outcomes A. B.
B. List Methods to accomplish each objective as A-1, A-2, A-3 … B-1, B-2 …

A / B	MONTH BEGIN END (C/D)	TIME (E)	PROJECT PERSONNEL (F)	SALARIES & WAGES (G)	FRINGE BENEFITS (H)	TOTAL (I)	CONSULTANTS TIME (J)	COST/WEEK (K)	TOTAL (L)	ITEM (M)	COST/ITEM (N)	QUANTITY (O)	TOT. COST (P)	SUB-TOTAL TOTAL I.L.P (Q)	MILESTONES ITEM (R)	DATE (S)
Objective A: Increase Educational Cooperation of Teachers, Parents & Students 25% as Measured on The Educational Practices Survey in 12 months at a cost of $																
A-1 Develop the Responsible Educational Practices Survey With the Advisory Committee.	1/2	4	Proj. Dir-PD Smith	West	State	U.	2	1000	2000	micro/word perfect			2500			
a. Write questions and develop a scale of responsibility for parents, teachers & students			2 Grad students (GS)	"	"	"	2	500	1000	printer/modem / phone expense			175 / 150			
A-2 Administer the survey to the target population.	2/3	4	2 GS	"	"	"	4	500	2000							
a. develop procedure		4	PD	"	"	"	4	1000	4000							
b. get human subjects approval thru West State University																
c. graduate students to administer survey		4	2 GS	"	"	"	4	500	2000	travel allowance			800			
d. input survey data		*4	Sec'y	800	160	*960				modem/phone expense			150			
e. develop results		1	PD	West	State	U.	1	1000	1000	micro processor			---			
A-3 Develop Curriculum	3/6															
a. review results of pre-test given to parents, students & teachers		1	PD	"	"	"	1	1000	1000							
b. develop a curriculum on responsibility concepts in education for each group (includes workbook & video on each area of curriculum)		5 / *8	PD / Sec'y	" / 1600	" / 320	" / *1920	5	1000	5000	layot & print			1250			
o responsible use of time		8	Senior High Video Club – Using Jones Corp. Video Facility							workbooks / blank tapes / video studio	10 / 2 / 5000	200 / 20 / 5 hrs	2000* / 40 / 25000*			
o homework responsibility o communication skills o developing contract for change										camera edit character generation						
A-4 Promote and Carry-Out Program	6/12	24 / 24	PD / Sec'y	West / 4800	State / 960	U / *5760	24	1000	24000							
a. use advisory group to announce program																
b. public service spots on radio and television																
c. develop & send home a program																
d. schedule meetings with parents																
e. develop a student video										video camera	1000	6	6000*			

TOTAL DIRECT COSTS OR COSTS REQUESTED FROM FUNDER ▶	0	42000		5065	47065	53% ◀ % OF TOTAL
MATCHING FUNDS, IN-KIND CONTRIBUTIONS, OR DONATED COSTS ▶	8640	0		33000	41640	47% ◀
TOTAL COSTS ▶	8640	42000		38065	88705	100% ◀

CHAPTER ELEVEN

Developing Government Grant Proposals

Completing a federal government proposal is very much like filing an income tax return. As with tax returns, the directions are longer than the actual forms, but the forms are not really that complicated. If you have followed the Federal Grants Clock outlined in chapter 7, made preproposal contact, and secured a copy of a funded proposal, you have an advantage over the applicant who is trying to guess what the grantor wants.

A federal grant application must be completed exactly as prescribed in the rules. For example, CFDA 84.201 School Dropout Demonstration calls for 30 double-spaced pages printed in a font of at least 12 characters per inch and allows for attachments.

The basic format and the specific order of the parts of a federal proposal are usually similar for all applications. In addition to providing an abstract, or summary, the prospective grantee is normally required to identify:

- the need,
- the plan to address the need,
- the key personnel who will operate the program,
- the budget,
- how the success of the project will be evaluated,
- the adequacy of resources,
- assurances, and
- attachments.

The points assigned to each area and the distribution of any additional or extra points are outlined in each agency's specific proposal guidelines.

The most important factor is that your proposal be easily understood by the reviewer. The reviewer must be able to read through the proposal rapidly, and the salient parts must be evident and well documented so that a point value can be assigned to each. Remember that your proposal will be read by a reviewer who most likely must evaluate each section according to a prescribed point system.

Proposal Abstract, or Summary

Some proposals require an abstract, or summary. Often the abstract must fit into a designated space or specific number of lines or pages. There is some controversy over *when* the abstract of the proposal should be written. Some experts believe it should be written *last*, when the grant writer can reflect on the completed proposal; others contend that writing the abstract *first* helps the grantee focus on preparing the proposal. Writing a detailed outline, then the proposal, and then an abstract that reviews the proposal usually works well.

Whether you write the abstract first or last, make sure it is in the required format. The abstract should provide a short, concise picture of the need, the objectives, the solution, and the evaluation.

In an effort to keep within the space limitations, some grant writers push the abstract to the margins and cram in as much information as possible. The result is usually difficult to read and very confusing. When you consider that the reviewer may have already read several proposals, the "crammed" abstract may set a negative tone for the entire proposal and lead to a low score.

Review the following abstract and consider whether it sets the stage properly. Ask yourself if it:

- shows that the grantseeker has a command of the need,

- shows that the project has measurable objectives,

- provides a synopsis of the methods, and

- presents the proposal's main points in an interesting manner.

> This project will identify those students at risk for dropping out, will intervene and provide the motivation and tools necessary to complete their high school education, and will encourage post secondary education and/or training. Over a three year period, this project will extend services to 450 students including 5 elementary programs which feed into 3 middle schools which, in turn, feed into 2 high school programs. Activities in this project will increase coping and daily living skills through classroom instruction, utilize community volunteers to tutor students and act as role models, increase awareness and incentive through two field trips, as well as track school attendance and classroom progress acting as a mediator between teachers, parents and students to resolve problems as they arise.

While not a wonderful example, this abstract does indicate that services will be extended to 450 students, five elementary programs, and three middle schools. In addition, it provides a rough idea of the types of activities aimed at keeping students in school. However, it does not even *hint* at the need or give any measurement indicators or criteria for success. Also, based on the abstract, the project seems geared to high schools, which makes one wonder why elementary and middle schools are even mentioned. But before we get too critical, we should note that the project summarized in this abstract was funded for approximately $97,000!

The Needs Statement

This section may be referred to as the "Search of Relevant Literature," the "Extent of the Need," or the "Problem." One federal program refers to the needs statement as the "Criterion: Extent to which the project meets specific needs recognized in the statute that authorized the program, including consideration of the needs addressed by the project; how the needs were identified; how the needs will be met; and the benefits to be gained by meeting the needs."

One successful grantee responded to this criterion with a description of the extent of the need that included the following:

1. **Target Area** — Where the applicant was located and data that identified a significant needs population in the student body.

2. **Need for Services** — What school programs were available and the gap between "what was" and "what should be."

86

3. How the Needs Would Be Met — A general description of what was to be done.

4. Benefits to Be Gained — The anticipated positive outcomes of the project.

When you are developing the needs section, you should take into consideration the type of reviewer who will be reading the proposal application. The needs section should be motivating and compelling. It must demonstrate that the applicant has credibility and a command of the current literature in the field. Many excellent proposals lose crucial points when the grantee fails to command the respect of the reviewer because he or she overlooks the needs section and places all of the emphasis on the project description and plan of operation.

The following "extent of the need" has been taken from a grant funded by the Department of Education for dropout prevention.[1]

> The target population to be served by the project has experienced low academic achievement, high public-assistance rates, high dropout rates, linguistic and cultural differences, geographic isolation, and inaccessibility to existing career and training information. These conditions have combined to create high unemployment, underemployment, poor self-image, and a resultant low standard of living among these people. Astin's study of college attrition clearly identifies family income as a significant factor which negatively impacts student success in post secondary education and contributes to high dropout rates. Astin does note, however, that this correlation is influenced by such other "mediation" factors as ability, motivation, financial concerns, and parental education.
>
> . . . The target population occupies a rural mountainous and desert region covering over 8,000 square miles, which is larger than the combined area of Delaware, Rhode Island and Connecticut.
>
> . . . It is pertinent to note that 79.3% of the active job applicants are ethnic minority and that 63.5% had less than a high school diploma.[2]

Facts like those presented in this excerpt tell the reviewer and the federal staff that the writer knows how things are. Including statistics in the needs section of a proposal shows a command of the situation and can make a positive impression, unlike "grant- loser statements" such as:

- "Everyone knows the need for . . ."
- "Current statistics show . . ."
- "It is a shame our students do not have . . ."
- "You can't believe the number of times . . ."
- "Several (Many, An increasing number of, and so on) students . . ."

When reviewers read such weak, banal statements, they take their frustration out on the scoring sheet, and the grantseeker loses valuable points. A strong needs statement requires facts, studies, and references, and it takes commitment and hard work to gather these. But remember, you will be repaid in grants success!

---

[1] Proposal: Four Corners School, College and University Partnership Program, Submitted to U.S. Department of Education, Division of Student Services, CDFA 84-204, by San Juan School District College of Eastern Utah — San Juan Campus, Utah Navajo Development Council, July 9, 1988.
[2] Alexander W. Astin, *Preventing Students from Dropping Out,* San Francisco: Jossey Bass, 1977.

Plan of Operation

Your government application may refer to this section as the "Plan of Operation," "Objectives and Methods," or "Project Methodology." The purpose of this section is to describe an organized solution to the need and problem you have identified.

Chapter 9 outlined how to construct behavioral/measurable objectives. By reviewing a previously funded proposal you can get a good idea of how the grantor prefers the plan of operation to be presented.

Review the following sample objectives. They were taken from a proposal for an early intervention dropout program. Keep in mind that the proposal was funded for $750,000!

1. 1,500 kindergarten through sixth grade at-risk students will benefit from the District's effort to institutionalize instructional improvement and variation by comprehensively upgrading all instructional and support services. This will include: attendance monitoring and immediate follow-up on absences; ombudsmen and advocates for students; junior high at-risk student tutoring of early grade at-risk students; extended school day programs; and off-site activities.

2. Seventy-five kindergarten through sixth grade teachers and two paraprofessionals will receive training on topics such as: implementation of effective school postulates, individualizing instruction, thematic instruction, ombudsmen and advocates for students, the city as a resource, training parents, managing at-risk student programs, and understanding the needs of ethnic minority (especially Hispanic American) and low income students.

3. Approximately 500 parents of at-risk students will attend 30 to 60 hours of project-sponsored activities focusing on issues such as: basic literacy, parenting, how to help your child with homework, English as a second language, and social issues information about: drug and alcohol abuse, AIDS, teenage pregnancy, and suicide.

4. The results of this program will be publicized and disseminated. Strategies will include: a recruitment video, a video that showcases the progress and achievements of students, a program brochure, TV spot announcements, and presentations at community events.

Do these objectives describe *what* will be accomplished or *how* the project will be done? For three-quarters of a million dollars, we should be told *what area* we can expect to see change in, and *how much change* we can expect.

Just because an objective contains numbers does not mean it is well constructed. For example, the above objectives tell us the *number* of parents to be trained but do not give us information on what the parents will do differently as a result of the training or what impact the parental training will have on children staying in school.

The following objective has been taken from another project funded by the Department of Education under a different program. It demonstrates the measurable component of an objective much more effectively.

By June 1, 1989, at least 65% of all students enrolled in the academic year program will improve at least 1.5 grade levels in mathematics, language mechanics, language expression, and reading ability as documented by pre-post Comprehensive Tests of Basic Skills scores.

Methods/Activities

Review chapter 10 on developing a Project Planner. The Project Planner will encourage an organized approach to developing your proposed plan. Whether you utilize the Project Planner or not, your proposal will be evaluated on the thoroughness and clarity of the steps prescribed. Again, a copy of a previously funded proposal will give you insight on how successful past grantees have organized this section of their proposals.

There are many ways to present objectives and methods. For instance, in the following example, the successful grantseeker first presents a main objective, then a subobjective or process objective, and finally the methodologies.

OBJECTIVE 3: UPGRADE BASIC SKILLS

PROCESS OBJECTIVE 3.1: Students will be counseled and tutored during the academic year program to meet their individual academic needs and overcome areas of deficiency.

Methodologies:

a) Deficiencies of participants will be documented through use of CTBS scores, transcripts, and interviews with teachers, parents, students and counselors. Through this process and individual education, a plan will be prepared based on areas of strengths, but particularly on areas of weakness in which the student needs help. This will be in the form of a contract which the student and counselor will sign to agree to work together to strengthen the academic skills which need improvement.

b) The counselor will schedule bi-weekly, after-school tutoring and counseling sessions to provide academic assistance as well as emotional support.

Personnel Responsible: Project counselors, tutors, and teachers from each high school.

Resources: Textbooks, testing and teaching materials, media centers of each high school.

Quality of Key Personnel

This section tells the reviewer how qualified your project staff is to meet the objectives and close the gap between what is and what ought to be.

One dilemma that proposal developers face is that their key personnel often have not been hired by the time the proposal is submitted. In this case, the proposal should clearly show that capable staff can be found. Remember, reviewers who have worked their way through most of a proposal will want to be certain of the quality of the individuals who will implement the project.

Review the following sample taken from a funded Department of Education grant.

Criterion: The quality of the key personnel the applicant plans to use in the project. Staff will consist of a full-time project director, a full-time assistant project director, four part-time regular school year counselors, four full-time summer counselors, eight college and peer tutors, 12 part-time instructors, and a full-time secretary. Inasmuch as project staff have not been identified at this time, resumes are not included. The partnership would like to affirm that no problems are anticipated in acquiring qualified, experienced, highly competent personnel. At least one week will be scheduled at the beginning of the project for the orientation of staff to the goals, objectives, plan of operation, etc.

Do you feel confident that this applicant has the expertise necessary to conduct this project? Does the grantee's statement that "no problems are anticipated in acquiring qualified . . . personnel" make you feel comfortable? This is like betting on a horse you know nothing about, simply because someone assures you that it will be a winner. Every grantor wants to know the track record of people who will be working on the project.

In the example, the applicant could have stated that the project director would be reporting to Dr. Smith, who is currently responsible for managing *X* million dollars. For your information, however, the prospective grantee did at least follow the key personnel criterion with a detailed description of the major positions mentioned in the body of the proposal.

Note that many government grantors look for the *appropriate* use of personnel. If you are thinking about *minimally involving* one outstanding person in *many grants,* you should be aware that some funders ask for an outline of the time each staff member will commit to the project and that some federal grants require that the project director or principal investigator commit a certain percentage of his or her time to the project. In other words, one outstanding and well-known individual should not commit 2 percent of his or her time to 50 different projects!

Budget and Cost Effectiveness

While each federal program's proposal requirements may differ, all applications will require a budget. In most cases, the amount of the proposal (the dollar request) will be divided by the number of students who will benefit from the project so that the federal program officer can arrive at a cost per student served. One of the primary concerns of a reviewer is that the budget request be reasonable, based on the steps outlined in the proposal. For example, if a project is meant to be a model for other schools, it must be affordable enough to be replicated.

The following sample has been taken from a copy of a successful federally funded proposal. Note that in the actual proposal, the references to the cost per student served have been omitted to prevent the reader from calculating a formula he or she believes to result in a "preferred" cost figure.

REASONABLENESS OF BUDGET

Criterion: Costs are reasonable in relation to the objective of the project.

Salaries and benefits are based upon institutional schedules and policies. Supplies have been computed on the basis of local vendor prices. Travel and communication costs in such a geographically isolated location may appear to be rather extensive. These have been kept to a minimum with rates on institutional polices.

The overall cost per participant from federal funds amounts to $_____ the first year, decreasing to $_____ the second year, and $_____ the third year. The budget is reasonable and cost effective, particularly considering the geographic isolation of the target area.

A budget narrative may also be required. A budget narrative is an explanation of how the salaries, consultant services, equipment, and materials are related to the completion of each method or activity.

The Department of Education's most common budget information form for nonconstruction projects is Standard Form (SF)-424A. If you have completed a Project

Planner (see chapter 10), you already have all the information you need to complete the SF-424A or any other form the federal grantor may require. The preferred budget form will be included in your federal application package.

If possible, review the budget and cash forecast format of a successfully funded proposal.

Evaluation

If you developed your objectives according to the methods suggested in chapter 9, you have already outlined your basic steps for evaluation. Most projects demand some sort of preassessment survey so that baseline data can be gathered. After the completion of the intervention steps or the model project, the original baseline data can be compared with posttest evaluation data to demonstrate change in the target population or problem.

Using outside or external consultants to evaluate a project is looked upon by many reviewers as a positive step since this may encourage an unbiased, independent evaluation. Discuss this important section of your proposal with your prospective grantor to gather as much insight as possible into their evaluation preferences.

The evaluation section of your proposal must clearly delineate:

- what will be evaluated,
- when the pre- and postevaluations will occur,
- how much change is predicted,
- who will perform the evaluation, and
- how much the evaluation component will cost.

In the example provided on the Sample Project Planner (see chapter 10), West State University was included so that the grantee did not end up evaluating its own work. By including a few West State University professors in the proposal the grantee also built credibility and demonstrated the efficient use of available local resources. Utilizing West State University's computer resources and graduate students in the evaluation also demonstrated the cost effectiveness of the grantee's proposal.

Adequacy of Resources

The information in this section should be included in every proposal whether or not the funding source requests it because it lets the funder know why they should make a grant to *your* school. You need to identify what makes your school a more logical choice for funding than any other school in your area. By focusing on the problem and your proposed solution, you will make your school the strongest candidate for receiving the grant.

The areas that most federal grantors and reviewers are influenced by include equipment, supplies, and facilities.

- **Equipment** — Demonstrate that you have enough *standard* office equipment (desks, chairs, and so on) to support the additional staff called for in your proposal. If your proposal calls for equipment that is not standard, such as modems and VCRs, and you are not requesting funds from the grantor to purchase these items, make it clear in your proposal that such equipment is being *donated* by you, the grantee, to the project. Your assurance that this equipment is available to support your project when it is funded demonstrates that you have adequate resources.

- **Supplies/Materials** — Any supplies and/or materials that you will be making available should also be noted. This will help build your case.
- **Facilities** — Describe the facilities that will be used to support the project, especially unique or different types of facilities such as computer labs, swimming pools, and so on. If your proposal involves another organization, show how its facilities and yours will be jointly used or shared to ensure the successful completion of the project.

Assurances

Your school officials will be required to provide signed assurances that the project will abide by a myriad of federal rules and regulations. Assurances deal with a wide range of issues, from drug-free workplaces to political lobbying. Your district's main office has probably signed assurances in the past and will be able to assist you in this process. For your general information, *The Catalogue of Federal Domestic Assistance* (the CFDA) outlines the required federal assurances.

One area of assurances that many school districts overlook is human subjects review. It is not necessary for your school district to organize an Institutional Review Board (IRB) to examine every federal proposal to assure that the human subjects involved are treated humanely; however, as a grantee you should develop a relationship with your local college or university so that you can arrange to have its IRB review and approve your federal proposals when appropriate.

Attachments

Reactive grantseeking limits the time available to write your proposal. Because of this, the applications of reactive grantseekers are often submitted without letters of support and agreement from cooperating organizations and community groups. This is a red flag to reviewers and often diminishes grantees' credibility and costs them valuable points. Be sure to take the time to gather your letters of support and agreement. Include them in your attachments.

When possible, it is a good idea to include your Project Planner also. Other attachments may include maps, pictures, a layout of your school's building, support data for the statement of need, surveys, and questionnaires.

Reviewers find it helpful when you reference the attachments in the body of your proposal and include a separate table of contents for the attachment section.

CHAPTER TWELVE

Improving and Submitting Your Federal Grant Application

The main purpose of this chapter is to provide you with a method of improving your federal proposal. The quality of your proposal will influence how reviewers and agency staff members view you and your school for many years to come. Just as teachers do not easily forget the first impression a student makes, reviewers and federal staff members do not easily forget the first impression made by a proposal.

If you and your peers extensively review your proposal before submitting it, you will feel more confident that you are sending the prospective grantor your best effort. And even if your proposal is not selected for funding, you can be certain it was rejected because of the competition and not because of careless mistakes.

If you're like most grantseekers, by now you are tired of the whole process and what you really want to do is submit your proposal and get it out of your life. But after coming this far you shouldn't throw away all your hard work by submitting a proposal that hasn't passed the last test — a mock review.

The beginning of this primer explained Festinger's Theory of Cognitive Dissonance and how you must view grantseeking from the funder's perspective rather than your own. You also need to *review* your proposal from the funder's perspective rather than your own.

The more you know about the review system used by federal agencies, the easier it will be to perform a mock review of your proposal. Through preproposal contact you should have learned how the granting agency selects reviewers, the reviewers' backgrounds, and which review system they follow. This information will ensure that your mock review is as much like the real review as possible.

The term *quality circle* best describes the process. Invite a small group of individuals who are dedicated to improving education to participate in the circle. The participants need not be experts in the grants area or in the particular subject area of your proposal. In fact, although you do want the members of the quality circle to mirror the types of reviewers on the real federal review committee, you should also invite several individuals with a fresh outlook to participate. For example, ask a business leader from your Grants Advisory Group, a college student, a secretary, and/or an accountant to be mock reviewers. These many different perspectives will give your quality circle a better chance of uncovering all or most of your proposal's weaknesses and strengths.

Either telephone individuals or ask them in person to participate. Brief them on the general approach you want them to take. It is important to begin by stating that you want to submit the best possible proposal and that a thorough review by a quality circle will help you achieve that goal. You should also let them know that you, your close associates, and your

SAMPLE LETTER INVITING INDIVIDUAL TO PARTICIPATE IN FEDERAL PROPOSAL QUALITY CIRCLE

Date

Name
Address

Dear ___________________:

I would like to take this opportunity to follow up on our conversation to secure your input in helping our school district submit the very best grant proposal possible. We are asking that you review the enclosed proposal from the point of view of a federal reviewer. The attached materials will help you role-play the actual manner in which this proposal will be evaluated.

Please read the information on the reviewers' backgrounds and the scoring system and limit the time you spend reading the proposal to the time constraints that the real reviewers will observe. A Quality Circle Scoring Worksheet has been provided to assist you in recording your scores and comments.

A meeting of all the mock reviewers comprising our quality circle has been scheduled for [date _______________]. Please bring this worksheet with you to the meeting. The meeting will last less than one hour. Its purpose is to analyze the scores and brainstorm suggestions to improve the proposal.

Sincerely,

Name
Phone Number

Grants Advisory Group members are so involved in the proposal that you need a fresh perspective. Tell them that you will be sending them a package that includes a description of the types of reviewers and the point or scoring system that will be used. Assure them that they do not have to be experts in the subject area but that they must make every attempt to read the proposal from the real reviewers' point of view. Use the sample letter in figure 12.1 to invite individuals to participate in your quality circle.

Each federal agency that makes grants follows a different proposal review system. For instance, the National Science Foundation's system is very different from that of the National Endowment for the Humanities, and the latter is much different from the system used by the Department of Education. The fact that proposal-review systems vary in selection criteria and scoring emphasizes the need for preproposal contact with the funder and early data gathering about the review process.

The Education Department uses a review system known as EDGAR (Education Department General Administrative Regulations). Not all programs in the Education Department follow EDGAR; some have their own published regulations with a specific set of criteria. However, if the program does not have a set of *published* guidelines, you can assume they follow EDGAR.

EDGAR's main areas of evaluation include:

1. How the proposed project meets the purposes of the authorizing statute
2. The extent of the need for the project
3. How the plan of operation meets the need
4. The availability of qualified key personnel to implement the plan
5. Whether the budget is cost effective and realistic with the respect to the plan of operation
6. How the plan's progress in meeting the objectives will be evaluated
7. Whether the applicant possesses sufficient resources to house the project and support the plan

To help your volunteers review and evaluate your proposal from the proper perspective, you may wish to provide them with the Selection Criteria Overview and Scoring Distribution in figures 12.2 and 12.3.

Try to obtain the following information from the granting agency:

- where and how the review occurs,
- the average time reviewers spend reading each proposal, and
- the number of proposals each reviewer is responsible for evaluating.

At the very least, you *must* give your quality circle members the point system and time constraints they should abide by. Volunteer reviewers often want to do such a good job that in their zeal, they spend much more time reviewing your proposal than the real reviewers will.

Ask the volunteers to read your proposal and to designate with an asterisk those areas they think the reviewer will like and those they think will be viewed negatively. Obviously, the negative areas should be improved prior to submission.

Send or give your volunteer reviewers the Quality Circle Scoring Worksheet in figure 12.4 and any other information you can gather that will assist them in their role playing. For example, information on last year's grantees may be useful, especially if the grantee mix is likely to remain the same.

You can perform the review by mail or ask the volunteers to get together for a short meeting to review the scores and discuss the proposal's positive and negative points. The members of the circle may not want to hurt your feelings by criticizing the proposal in your presence, so ask a friend to facilitate the meeting for you.

Be sure to remind your volunteer reviewers to mention your proposal's positive areas in their evaluations. In most cases, individuals tend to focus on the negatives, although it's also important for you to know what parts of your proposal looked "good" to the volunteer reviewers.

Review the scores each section of your proposal received. Based on the volunteers' scores and comments, identify the areas of your proposal that need to be improved and those that should remain the same.

Submission

The Standard Form (SF) 424 (fig. 12.5) must be attached to the front of your federal grant application or proposal. Instructions for its completion have also been included (fig. 12.6).

Do not bind your proposal or staple it together unless you have received permission to do so by the federal funder. Federal funders usually prefer grantseekers to submit their proposals with pressure tension clips so that forms can be added or removed as needed.

Figure 12.2

SELECTION CRITERIA OVERVIEW

Meeting the Purposes of the Authorizing Statute (5 pts)

1) What are the purposes of the authorizing statute?

2) What are the objectives of this project?

3) How will these objectives further the purposes of the authorizing statute?

Extent of Need for the Project (25 pts)

1) What needs are outlined by the authorizing statute?

2) What needs does the applicant identify?

3) How did the applicant identify those needs, i.e., what specific documentation or evidence does the application offer to support the applicant's assessment of need?

4) Are the needs identified by the applicant consistent with the purposes of the authorizing statute?

5) Does the applicant identify too many or too few needs for the proposed time frame and resources of the project?

6) Are the outlined needs well defined so that the project can be focused on them, or are the outlined needs very generic?

Plan of Operation (20 pts)

1) Do the project objectives serve the purposes of the authorizing statute?

2) How well is the project designed? Are project objectives consistent with stated needs? Are project activities consistent with project objectives? Are project objectives measurable?

3) How will the applicant use its resources and personnel to achieve each objective?

4) Has the applicant developed an effective management plan that will ensure proper and efficient administration of the project?

5) Do project milestones represent a logical progression of times and tasks?

6) Does the applicant propose a realistic time schedule for accomplishing objectives?

7) Will the proposed activities accomplish the project's objectives successfully?

8) Are the educational approaches planned based on sound research that indicates they will be successful for the population to be served?

9) Does the project have clearly developed provisions for providing equal access to eligible participants who are members of traditionally underrepresented groups (racial or ethnic minorities, women, handicapped persons, elderly persons)?

Quality of Key Personnel (15 pts)

1) Do the job descriptions adequately reflect skills needed to make the project work?

2) Are the duties of personnel clearly defined?

3) What relevant qualifications do the proposed personnel possess, especially the Project Director? (Focus on their experience and training in fields related to the objectives of the project, though other information may be considered.)

4) Will proposed personnel need to be trained for the project?

5) How much time will the proposed personnel actually devote to the project?

6) To what extent does the applicant encourage employment applications from members of traditionally underrepresented groups (ethnic or racial minorities, women, handicapped persons, elderly persons)?

Budget and Cost Effectiveness (10 pts)

1) Is the budget adequate to support the project's proposed activities?

2) Are overall project costs reasonable in relation to project objectives?

3) How much of the project's total cost is devoted to administrative costs?

4) Are budget items sufficiently justified?

5) Is the budget padded?

Evaluation Plan (15 pts)

1) Are the proposed methods of evaluation appropriate to the project?

2) Will the proposed evaluation be objective?

3) Will the proposed evaluation methods measure the effectiveness of project activities in meeting project objectives?

4) Will the evaluation plan produce valid and reliable data concerning the accomplishment of project objectives?

5) Does the evaluation plan measure the project's effect on the project audience?

Adequacy of Resources (10 pts)

1) Are the proposed facilities adequate for project purposes?

2) Is the proposed equipment adequate for project purposes?

3) Does the applicant have access to special sources of experience or expertise?

SCORING DISTRIBUTION WORKSHEET

Scoring

The numerical scores you assign to an application's response to the selection criteria must be consistent with the comments you write. Comments and scores should reflect the same overall assessment. You should never attempt to mitigate a negative comment with a positive score, or vice versa.

Comments indicate whether the application's response to the selection criteria is poor, adequate, or good; scores indicate *how* poor, adequate, or good. If 10 points are possible, 0–2 points is poor, 5–7 points is adequate, and 8–9 points is superior. Four points will indicate a response that is merely weak, whereas 8 points will indicate a response that is above average. Whatever amount of total points is possible, use the midpoint of the scale as adequate and choose your scores accordingly. Do not hesitate to use the full range of points. It is perfectly acceptable to assign a score of 10 or 1, for example. Your guiding rule should be consistency in rating.

Always go back and check your scores to make sure that you have written them correctly and used the appropriate point scale. You should also double-check the scores on the summary page of the Technical Review Form to make sure that they match the scores listed under each selection criterion and that the final total has been computed without error.

You may want to use the following table as a guide when assigning points:

Total	Poor	Weak	Adequate	Superior	Outstanding
25	0–8	9–12	13–19	20–23	24–25
20	0–6	7–9	10–15	16–18	19–20
15	0–4	5–7	8–11	12–13	14–15
10	0–2	3–4	5–7	8–9	10
5	0–1	2	3	4	5

Application Transmittal

Your federal application package will contain specific directions on how to transmit your proposal by mail or hand delivery to Washington, D.C.

The instructions in figure 12.7 have been taken from the Department of Education's federal guidelines. Note that granting agencies have different rules regarding transmittal. Always check to be sure you are following the correct process.

The main purpose of the proactive grants system is to be able to submit your proposal early, not just on time. If you submit your proposal early, the federal bureaucrats may think that you will also submit your reports early once you are funded. This is all to the good!

Signature

Your federal grant application cover letter and assurances must be signed by an authorized district representative. Your district grants office may help you procure the necessary signatures.

QUALITY CIRCLE SCORING WORKSHEET

The following information is being provided to assist you in reviewing the attached federal grant application/proposal.

The Setting — The proposals are read at:

_________ the reviewer's location

_________ the federal agency's location

_________ other site selected by the federal agency

The Time Factor

Number of proposals the reviewer evaluates: _________

Amount of time the reviewer spends evaluating each proposal: _________

Areas To Be Scored	Points/Area	Comments/Suggestions

Total Points for Proposal

What is the background and training of the evaluators? ___________________

____

____

____

What point system will be followed? _______________________________

____

____

____

How much time will be spent reviewing each proposal? ___________________

____

Use this space to note anything "special" that will affect proposal outcome.

____

____

____

____

Figure 12.5

OMB Approval No. 0348-0043

APPLICATION FOR FEDERAL ASSISTANCE

2. DATE SUBMITTED	Applicant Identifier
3. DATE RECEIVED BY STATE	State Application Identifier
4. DATE RECEIVED BY FEDERAL AGENCY	Federal Identifier

1. TYPE OF SUBMISSION:

Application	Preapplication
☐ Construction	☐ Construction
☐ Non-Construction	☐ Non-Construction

5. APPLICANT INFORMATION

Legal Name:

Organizational Unit:

Address (give city, county, state, and zip code):

Name and telephone number of the person to be contacted on matters involving this application (give area code)

6. EMPLOYER IDENTIFICATION NUMBER (EIN):

☐☐ — ☐☐☐☐☐☐☐

7. TYPE OF APPLICANT: (enter appropriate letter in box) ☐

A. State	H. Independent School Dist.
B. County	I. State Controlled Institution of Higher Learning
C. Municipal	J. Private University
D. Township	K. Indian Tribe
E. Interstate	L. Individual
F. Intermunicipal	M. Profit Organization
G. Special District	N. Other (Specify): ________

8. TYPE OF APPLICATION:

☒ New   ☐ Continuation   ☐ Revision

If Revision, enter appropriate letter(s) in box(es): ☐ ☐

A. Increase Award   B. Decrease Award   C. Increase Duration

D. Decrease Duration   Other (specify):

____

9. NAME OF FEDERAL AGENCY:

U. S. Department of Education

10. CATALOG OF FEDERAL DOMESTIC ASSISTANCE NUMBER: 8 4 . 2 0 1

C.D. 3/26/92
TITLE: School Dropout Demonstration Assistance Program

11. DESCRIPTIVE TITLE OF APPLICANT'S PROJECT:

12. AREAS AFFECTED BY PROJECT (cities, counties, states, etc.):

13. PROPOSED PROJECT:

Start Date	Ending Date

14. CONGRESSIONAL DISTRICTS OF:

a. Applicant	b. Project

15. ESTIMATED FUNDING:

a. Federal	$	.00
b. Applicant	$	.00
c. State	$	.00
d. Local	$	.00
e. Other	$	.00
f. Program Income	$	.00
g. TOTAL	$	.00

16. IS APPLICATION SUBJECT TO REVIEW BY STATE EXECUTIVE ORDER 12372 PROCESS?

a. YES. THIS PREAPPLICATION/APPLICATION WAS MADE AVAILABLE TO THE STATE EXECUTIVE ORDER 12372 PROCESS FOR REVIEW ON:

DATE_____________________

b. NO. ☐ PROGRAM IS NOT COVERED BY E.O. 12372

☐ OR PROGRAM HAS NOT BEEN SELECTED BY STATE FOR REVIEW

17. IS THE APPLICANT DELINQUENT ON ANY FEDERAL DEBT?

☐ Yes   If "Yes," attach an explanation.   ☐ No

18. TO THE BEST OF MY KNOWLEDGE AND BELIEF, ALL DATA IN THIS APPLICATION/PREAPPLICATION ARE TRUE AND CORRECT, THE DOCUMENT HAS BEEN DULY AUTHORIZED BY THE GOVERNING BODY OF THE APPLICANT AND THE APPLICANT WILL COMPLY WITH THE ATTACHED ASSURANCES IF THE ASSISTANCE IS AWARDED

a. Typed Name of Authorized Representative	b. Title	c. Telephone number
d. Signature of Authorized Representative		e. Date Signed

Previous Editions Not Usable

Standard Form 424   (REV 4-88)

Authorized for Local Reproduction

INSTRUCTIONS FOR THE SF 424

This is a standard form used by applicants as a required facesheet for preapplications and applications submitted for Federal assistance. It will be used by Federal agencies to obtain applicant certification that States which have established a review and comment procedure in response to Executive Order 12372 and have selected the program to be included in their process, have been given an opportunity to review the applicant's submission.

Item: **Entry:**

1. Self-explanatory.

2. Date application submitted to Federal agency (or State if applicable) & applicant's control number (if applicable).

3. State use only (if applicable).

4. If this application is to continue or revise an existing award, enter present Federal identifier number. If for a new project, leave blank.

5. Legal name of applicant, name of primary organizational unit which will undertake the assistance activity, complete address of the applicant, and name and telephone number of the person to contact on matters related to this application.

6. Enter Employer Identification Number (EIN) as assigned by the Internal Revenue Service.

7. Enter the appropriate letter in the space provided.

8. Check appropriate box and enter appropriate letter(s) in the space(s) provided:

   —"New" means a new assistance award.

   —"Continuation" means an extension for an additional funding/budget period for a project with a projected completion date.

   —"Revision" means any change in the Federal Government's financial obligation or contingent liability from an existing obligation.

9. Name of Federal agency from which assistance is being requested with this application.

10. Use the Catalog of Federal Domestic Assistance number and title of the program under which assistance is requested.

11. Enter a brief descriptive title of the project. If more than one program is involved, you should append an explanation on a separate sheet. If appropriate (e.g., construction or real

Item: **Entry:**

property projects), attach a map showing project location. For preapplications, use a separate sheet to provide a summary description of this project.

12. List only the largest political entities affected (e.g., State, counties, cities).

13. Self-explanatory.

14. List the applicant's Congressional District and any District(s) affected by the program or project.

15. Amount requested or to be contributed during the first funding/budget period by each contributor. Value of in-kind contributions should be included on appropriate lines as applicable. If the action will result in a dollar change to an existing award, indicate *only* the amount of the change. For decreases, enclose the amounts in parentheses. If both basic and supplemental amounts are included, show breakdown on an attached sheet. For multiple program funding, use totals and show breakdown using same categories as item 15.

16. Applicants should contact the State Single Point of Contact (SPOC) for Federal Executive Order 12372 to determine whether the application is subject to the State intergovernmental review process.

17. This question applies to the applicant organization, not the person who signs as the authorized representative. Categories of debt include delinquent audit disallowances, loans and taxes.

18. To be signed by the authorized representative of the applicant. A copy of the governing body's authorization for you to sign this application as official representative must be on file in the applicant's office. (Certain Federal agencies may require that this authorization be submitted as part of the application.)

Figure 12.7

APPLICATION TRANSMITTAL INSTRUCTIONS

An application for an award must be mailed or hand delivered by the closing date.

Applications Delivered by Mail

An application sent by mail must be addressed to the U.S. Department of Education, Application Control Center, Attention: CFDA Number __________, 400 Maryland Avenue SW, Washington, D.C. 20202-4725.

An application must show proof of mailing consisting of one of the following:

> (1) A legibly dated U.S. Postal Service postmark.

> (2) A legible mail receipt with the date of mailing stamped by the U.S. Postal Service.

> (3) A dated shipping label, invoice, or receipt from a commercial carrier.

> (4) Any other proof of mailing acceptable to the U.S. Secretary of Education.

If an application is sent through the U.S. Postal Service, the Secretary does not accept either of the following as proof of mailing:

> (1) A private metered postmark, or

> (2) A mail receipt that is not dated by the U.S. Postal Service.

An applicant should note that the U.S. Postal Service does not uniformly provide a dated postmark. Before relying on this method, an applicant should check with the local post office.

An applicant is encouraged to use registered or at least first class mail.

Late applicants will be notified that their applications will not be considered.

Applications Delivered by Hand/Courier Service

An application that is hand delivered must be taken to the U.S. Department of Education, Application Control Center, Room 3633, General Services Administration National Capital Region, 7th and D Streets SW., Washington, D.C. 20202-4725.

The Application Control Center will accept deliveries between 8:00 a.m. and 4:30 p.m. (Washington, D.C.) daily, except Saturdays, Sundays, and federal holidays.

Individuals delivering applications must use the D Street entrance. Proper identification is necessary to enter the building.

In order for an application sent through a courier service to be considered timely, the courier service must be in receipt of the application on or before the closing date.

Intergovernmental Review of Federal Programs

The purpose of an intergovernmental review is to provide a mechanism for coordinating funds and projects and to reduce the chances of the federal government supporting a program that the state has decided is not part of its plan. Not all programs require an intergovernmental review, and not all states have the same reporting requirements. However, if an intergovernmental review is required, and your district has a grants office or a formal grants procedure, they will most likely handle the review.

If *you* must handle the review, contact your state's single point of contact to ensure that you comply with your state's requirements for coordinating your grant with other programs in your state. A list of State Single Points of Contact has been included for your convenience (fig. 12.8).

STATE SINGLE POINTS OF CONTACT

ALABAMA
Mrs. Moncell Thornell
State Single Point of Contact
Alabama Department of
 Economic & Community Affairs
3465 Norman Bridge Road
P.O. Box 250347
Montgomery, Alabama 36125-0347
Telephone: (205) 284-8905

ARIZONA
Ms. Janice Dunn
Arizona State Clearinghouse
3800 North Central Avenue
Fourteenth Floor
Phoenix, Arizona 85012
Telephone: (602) 280-1315

ARKANSAS
Mr. Joseph Gillespie
Manager, State Clearinghouse
Office of Intergovernmental Service
Department of Finance & Administration
P.O. Box 3278
Little Rock, Arkansas 72203
Telephone: (501) 371-1074

CALIFORNIA
Chris Kinne
Grants Coordinator
Office of Planning & Research
1400 Tenth Street
Sacramento, California 95814
Telephone: (916) 445-0613

COLORADO
State Single Point of Contact
State Clearinghouse
Division of Local Government
1313 Sherman Street, Room 520
Denver, Colorado 80203
Telephone: (303) 866-2156

CONNECTICUT
Under Secretary
Attn: Intergovernmental Review
 Coordinator
Comprehensive Planning Division
Office of Policy & Management
80 Washington Street
Hartford, Connecticut 06106-4459
Telephone: (203) 566-3410

DELAWARE
Ms. Francine Booth
State Single Point of Contact
Executive Department
Thomas Collins Building
Dover, Delaware 19903
Telephone: (302) 736-3326

DISTRICT OF COLUMBIA
Ms. Lovetta Davis
State Single Point of Contact
Executive Office of the Mayor
Office of Intergovernmental Relations
Room 416, District Building
1350 Pennsylvania Avenue, N.W.
Washington, D.C. 20004
Telephone: (202) 727-9111

FLORIDA
Ms. Janice L. Alcott
Director, Florida State Clearinghouse
Executive Office of the Governor
Office of Planning & Budgeting
The Capitol
Tallahassee, Florida 32399-0001
Telephone: (904) 488-8114

GEORGIA
Mr. Charles H. Badger
Administrator
Georgia State Clearinghouse
270 Washington Street, S.W.
Atlanta, Georgia 30334
Telephone: (404) 656-3855

HAWAII
Ms. Mary Lou Koayashi
Planning Program Manager
Office of State Planning
Office of the Governor
State Capitol - Room 406
Honolulu, Hawaii 96813
Telephone: (808) 548-5893
FAX (808) 548-8172

ILLINOIS
Jami Owens
State Single Point of Contact
Office of the Governor
State of Illinois
Springfield, Illinois 62706
Telephone: (217) 782-1671

INDIANA
Mr. Frank Sullivan
Budget Director
State Budget Agency
212 State House
Indianapolis, Indiana 46204
Telephone: (317) 232-5610

IOWA
Mr. Steven R. McCann
Division for Community Progress
Iowa Department of Economic
200 East Grand Avenue
Des Moines, Iowa 50309
Telephone: (515) 281-3725

KENTUCKY
Mr. Ronald W. Cook
Office of the Governor
Department of Local Government
2nd Floor, Capital Plaza Tower
Frankfort, Kentucky 40601
Telephone: (502) 564-2382

MARYLAND
Ms. Mary Abrams
Chief
Maryland State Clearinghouse
Department of State Planning
301 West Preston Street
Baltimore, Maryland 21201-2365

MASSACHUSETTS
State Single Point of Contact
Attn: Ms. Beverly Boyle
Executive Office of
 Communities & Development
100 Cambridge Street, Rm. 1803
Boston, Massachusetts 02202
Telephone: (617) 727-7001

MICHIGAN
Mr. Milton O. Waters
Director of Operations
Michigan Neighborhood Builders Alliance
Michigan Department of Commerce
Telephone: (517) 373-7111

Please direct correspondence to:
Manager, Federal Project Review
Michigan Department of Commerce
Michigan Neighborhood
 Builders Alliance
P.O. Box 30242
Lansing, Michigan 48909
Telephone: (517) 373-6223

MISSISSIPPI
Ms. Cathy Mallette
Clearinghouse Officer
Department of Finance & Administration
Office of Policy Development
421 West Pascagoula Street
Jackson, Mississippi 39203
Telephone: (601) 960-4280

MISSOURI
Ms. Lois Pohl
Federal Assistance Clearinghouse
Office of Administration
Division of General Services
P.O. Box 809
Room 430, Truman Building
Jefferson City, Missouri 65102
Telephone: (314) 751-4834

MONTANA
Ms. Deborah Staton
State Single Point of Contact
Intergovernmental Review
 Clearinghouse
c/o Office of Budget & Program Planning
Capitol Station
Room 202 - State Capitol
Helena, Montana 59620
Telephone: (406) 444-5522

NEVADA
Department of Administration
State Clearinghouse
Capitol Complex
Carson City, Nevada 89710
Attn: Mr. John B. Walker
Clearinghouse Coordinator

NEW HAMPSHIRE
Mr. Jeffery H. Taylor
Director
Office of State Planning
Attn: Intergovernmental Review
 Process/James E. Bieber
2 1/2 Beacon Street
Concord, New Hampshire 03301
Telephone: (603) 271-2155

NEW JERSEY
Mr. Andrew J. Jaskolka
State Review Process,
Department of Community Affairs
CN 814, Room 609
Trenton, New Jersey 08625-0814
Telephone: (609) 292-9025

NEW MEXICO
Ms. Aurelia M. Sandoval
State Budget Division, DFA
Rm. 190, Bataan Memorial Bldg.
Sante Fe, New Mexico 87503
Telephone: (505) 827-3640
Fax: (505) 827-3006

NEW YORK
New York State Clearinghouse
Division of the Budget
State Capitol
Albany, New York 12224
Telephone: (518) 474-1605

NORTH CAROLINA
Mrs. Chrys Baggett, Director
Intergovernmental Relations
Department of Administration
116 West Jones Street
Raleigh, North Carolina 27611
Telephone: (919) 733-0499

NORTH DAKOTA
Mr. Jim Boyd
State Single Point of Contact
Office of Intergovernmental Affairs
Office of Management & Budget
14th Floor, State Capitol
600 East Boulevard Avenue
Bismarck, North Dakota 58505–0170
Telephone: (701) 224-2094

OHIO
Mr. Larry Weaver
State Single Point of Contact
State/Federal Funds Coordinator
State Clearinghouse
Office of Budget & Management
30th East Broad Street, 34th Fl.
Columbus, Ohio 43266-0411
Telephone: (614) 466-0698

OKLAHOMA
Mr. Don Strain
State Single Point of Contact
Oklahoma Department of Commerce
Office of Federal Assistance
 Management
6601 Broadway Extension
Oklahoma City, Oklahoma 73116
Telephone: (405) 843-9770

OREGON
Attn: Ms. Delores Streeter
State Single Point of Contact
Intergovernmental Relation Division
State Clearinghouse
155 Cottage Street, N.E.
Salem, Oregon 97310
Telephone: (503) 373-1998

RHODE ISLAND
Mr. Daniel W. Varin
Single Point of Contact
Department of Administration
Division of Planning
1 Capitol Hill - Fourth Floor
Providence, Rhode Island
 02908-5870
Telephone: (401) 277-2656

SOUTH CAROLINA
Mr. Danny L. Cromer
State Single Point of Contact
Grant Services
Office of the Governor
1205 Pendleton Street, Rm. 477
Columbia, South Carolina 29201
Telephone: (803) 734-0493

SOUTH DAKOTA
Ms. Susan Comer
State Clearinghouse Coordinator
Office of the Governor
500 East Capitol
Pierre, South Dakota 57501
Telephone: (605) 773-3212

TENNESSEE
Mr. Charles Brown
State Single Point of Contact
State Planning Office
500 Charlotte Avenue
309 John Sevier Building
Nashville, Tennessee 37219
Telephone: (615) 741-1676

TEXAS
Mr. Tom Adams
Governor's Office of Budget & Planning
P.O. Box 12428
Austin, Texas 78711
Telephone: (512) 463-1778

UTAH
Utah State Clearinghouse
Office of Planning & Budget
Attn: Ms. Carolyn Wright
Room 116, State Capitol
Salt Lake City, Utah 84114
Telephone: (801) 538-1535

VERMONT
Mr. Bernard D. Johnson
Assistant Director
Office of Policy Research &
 Coordination
Pavilion Office Building
109 State Street
Montpelier, Vermont 05602
Telephone: (802) 828-3326

STATE SINGLE POINTS OF CONTACT

WASHINGTON
Ms. Marilyn Dawson
Washington Intergovernmental Review
  Process
Department of Community Development
9th and Columbia Building
Mail Stop GH-51
Olympia, Washington 98504-4151
Telephone: (206) 753-4978

WEST VIRGINIA
Mr. Fred Cutlip
Director
Community Development Division
Governor's Office of Community
  & Industrial Development
Building #6, Room 553
Charleston, West Virginia 25305
Telephone: (304) 348-4010

WISCONSIN
Mr. William C. Carey
Federal/State Relations Office
IGA Relations
101 South Webster Street
P.O. Box 7864
Milwaukee, Wisconsin 53707
Telephone: (608) 266-1741

Please direct correspondence and
questions to:
Mr. William C. Carey, Section Chief
Federal/State Relations Office
Wisconsin Department of
  Administration
Telephone: (608) 266-0267

WYOMING
Ms. Ann Redman
State Single Point of Contact
Wyoming State Clearinghouse
State Planning Coordinator's Office
Capitol Building
Cheyenne, Wyoming 82002
Telephone: (307) 777-7574

TERRITORIES

GUAM
Mr. Michael J. Reidy
Director
Bureau of Budget &
  Management Research
Office of the Governor
P.O. Box 2950
Agana, Guam 96910
Telephone: (671) 472-2285

**NORTHERN MARIANA
ISLANDS**
State Single Point of Contact
Planning & Budget Office
Office of the Governor
Saipan, CM
Northern Mariana Islands   96950

PUERTO RICO
Ms. Patria Custodio/
Mr. Israel Soto Marrero
Chairman/Director
Puerto Rico Planning Board
Minillas Government Center
P.O. Box 41119
San Juan, Puerto Rico 00940-9985
Telephone: (809) 727-4444

VIRGIN ISLANDS
Mr. Jose L. George
Director
Office of Management & Budget
Number 32 & 33 Kongens Gade
Charlotte Amalie, V.I. 00802
Telephone: (809) 774-0750

Private granting sources utilize a variety of terms to refer to the format in which proposals must be submitted. Foundations and corporations may ask that you request a grant by writing:

- a letter of inquiry,
- a letter proposal,
- a concept paper, or
- a preproposal letter.

But no matter how private grantors refer to it, you must develop a distinctly different proposal for each foundation and corporation. While you will encounter few private funders with application requirements that rival the federal government's, it is imperative that you follow any instructions you do receive. For example, limitations on number of pages and attachments must be observed.

The foundation and corporate grants marketplace is very different from the federal grants arena. Private grantors have few office workers, staff, and paid reviewers and seldom have a predetermined scoring system for proposal evaluation. Some of the larger foundation and corporate granting programs have a specified proposal format and hire experts in the field to review proposals, but they are relatively rare. In general, proposals submitted to foundations and corporations are read by board members or trustees who have a limited amount of time to spend reviewing hundreds of proposals. Many are not experts in the areas funded by the organization, and none are professional reviewers. They are decision makers. They know what their foundation or corporation is looking for, and they answer only to their fellow trustees or board members. They prefer short proposals that can be read rapidly. What this means is that your proposal must stimulate their interest right from the beginning and be able to sustain it. The best way to show the respect that the reader's time deserves is to demonstrate that you have purposefully selected their organization and have constructed a tailored approach based upon their needs.

The biggest mistake you can make in pursuing grants from foundations and corporations is to use the "shotgun" approach — one proposal fits all. The reader can see at a glance that the same proposal has been "shotgunned" to a list of prospective funders. The "shotgun" approach tells the funding source that their foundation or corporation was lumped together with others and that their individual values and needs were ignored for the convenience of the grantwriter. The forethought and effort you have invested thus far in studying the proactive grants process mean that you will not be shotgunning but using a telescopic lens to zero in on your most likely funder. Remember, you are striving for a 40 percent to 50 percent success rate. Your foundation or corporate proposal is not a direct-mail fund-raising piece that you expect less than a 1 percent return on. The grantors you solicit represent one of the most prestigious groups of potential supporters for your school. You must present them with your *best* effort, not the most convenient or easiest.

The Letter Proposal

The most common type of a proposal to a foundation or corporation is written as a letter and submitted on the applicant's stationery or letterhead. Most private funders limit letter proposals to two or three pages and do not allow attachments.

The main components of a letter proposal include:

1. an introductory paragraph stating your reason for writing,
2. a paragraph describing why you selected this particular grantor,
3. a needs paragraph,
4. a solution paragraph,
5. a request for funds paragraph,
6. a uniqueness paragraph indicating why *your* school should receive the grant instead of another school,
7. a closing paragraph,
8. signatures, and
9. attachments (if allowed).

Write a draft of your proposal by following the preceding outline. Try to stick to the outline, writing each paragraph in the order suggested; then edit and rearrange if necessary. Remember, the arrangement of the paragraphs should be geared to the grantor's point of view. Your proposal should follow an order that will sustain the funder's interest. Be sure to look at your letter proposal from the perspective of a reader who does not know everything you know about your proposed project.

The Sections of a Letter Proposal

1. INTRODUCTION

In this section refer to any linkages or friends who have already talked to the foundation or corporate board members/trustees on your behalf. Avoid focusing on yourself. Do not begin by stating, "We are writing to you because we need . . ." The funding source knows you are writing to them, and what *you* need is not their primary concern. What *they* value and need is their focus. Therefore, place the emphasis on them. For example: "John Smith suggested that I contact the Jones Foundation with an exciting project that deals with _______________, an area about which our school and your board share a deep concern."

2. WHY YOU SELECTED THEM OR HOW YOU KNOW THEY ARE INTERESTED IN THE EDUCATIONAL NEED ADDRESSED IN YOUR PROPOSAL

Demonstrate that you have done your homework by showing off your knowledge. For foundations, analyze your research. For example, by closely examining a foundation's IRS tax return you may be able to develop an interesting fact or statistic that is not obvious and does not appear in a foundation resource publication. You could also cite an outstanding grant recipient or program previously funded by the foundation to show your familiarity with their granting pattern and history. For instance, if a foundation's tax return indicates that approximately 25 percent of their grants are related to children, you could add two years together and say something like:

> My research indicates that in a recent two-year period, the Smith Foundation made ________ grants totaling over ____________ dollars for projects focusing on children and their ability to compete. Your granting pattern has prompted us to submit to you this proposal for improving our faculty's ability to involve parents in the education of their children attending Neighborville Middle School.

Corporate grants information is more difficult to collect and analyze than foundation grants information because corporations do not have to make their records available to the public. For corporate grantors it may be necessary to gather insights through linkages, preproposal contact, or company workers who have volunteered to help you. For instance: "Harry Higgs, chairperson of our volunteer group and your employee, has stated that the Jones Corporation places a high value on quality education for young people."

In general, this section of your letter proposal should make the funder realize that:

- you did your homework,
- you believe they are special and unique, and
- they should keep reading.

Although the "request for funds" usually appears later in the letter proposal, you can put it in this section if you choose to. This avoids the problem of having a grantor get very interested in your project only to find that the amount you ultimately request is not realistic. If you decide to put your grant request in this section, introduce its anticipated size by comparing your grant amount to the foundation's or corporation's average grant size for that subject area. For example: "Our research has shown that your average grant size for (subject area) is $26,500. It is with this knowledge that we encourage you to consider this grant for $25,000."

3. THE NEED FOR YOUR PROJECT

Do not describe your project in this section. Unfortunately, overzealous grantseekers have a tendency to jump right into a description of what they want to do. You should describe *your* project and solution *after* the funding source understands the need for *any* project or solution.

Review your research on the funding source. Remember, you are trying to demonstrate that there is a gap between what is and what ought to be. The more you know about the funder's values and perspective, the better you can select the appropriate documentation of need. The needs section must:

- be motivating and compelling enough to sustain the funder's interest,
- demonstrate that you have a command of the literature and the state of the art concerning the problem, and
- appeal to the perspective and interests of the private grantor.

Review the grants pattern of the funder. Knowing the types of projects they have funded in the past and where the projects were implemented will give you valuable insight and allow you to select and tailor the data you present in the needs section. While federal and state grantors and reviewers expect statistics, research references, and quotations, foundation and corporate readers may be more motivated by an example, a story, or a case study. For instance, the needs section of a letter proposal to a foundation may include something like the following.

National studies have demonstrated that children watch television an average of ______ hours per day. A survey of the fourth graders at ABC Elementary School showed that their television viewing surpassed the national average by 20%. One possible reason for this disparity could be that the children from ABC Elementary School spend more time alone than many children. One fourth grader surveyed said, "I ride a bus for one hour to get home after school. I'm lonely and tired and my mom doesn't get home until late, so TV is my friend—and a lot better friend than my brother! People who say TV is violent have never lived with my brother."

It is important to determine what type of needs documentation the prospective grantor will find the most motivating. Does the funding source's distribution of past grants show any specific geographic preferences? What types of grantees have been supported in the past? Can this information help you select the "right" data, studies, or examples to document the need?

In respect to corporate funders, review what you know about them. Where do they have company plants or centers of operation? How can the problem addressed in your proposal affect their marketplace and products? Because corporations need well-educated workers, you will find that they are normally concerned with the educational achievement of their employees and their employees' children.

4. SOLUTION — WHAT CAN BE DONE TO SOLVE THIS PROBLEM

It is often difficult to construct this section of the letter proposal in the limited space available. The previous paragraphs of the letter proposal focus on the grantor, and normally knowledge of the funding source is limited. But at this point in the proposal it is time to describe your project or, in other words, to summarize your solution. Naturally, you have much more information than you can fit in a few short paragraphs. The challenge is to decide what to include and what to exclude. What you must not do is describe your solution in such great detail that you confuse the prospective funding source and prevent them from understanding the overall concept. This could cause you to lose funding altogether. Remember, you can always supply the funder with more information on request. The object of this section is to provide the prospective grantor with a *basic* understanding of the solution you have chosen to meet the needs you have outlined. To do so, ask yourself what you would want to see in the solution if you were the grantor.

The Project Planner may make it easier to keep your project summary short. If you have developed a Project Planner (see chapter 10) you may want to *attach it to* your proposal or *include it in* your proposal. Be sure that attachments are allowed before you include the Project Planner as an attachment. If attachments are not allowed, you could make your Project Planner page two of a three-page letter proposal. The Project Planner is a useful inclusion because it clearly shows the relationship between activities or methods and the accomplishment of the objectives. The Project Planner also provides an excellent basis for the budget section that will follow, particularly when you consider that it can summarize five or more pages of narrative on one spreadsheet!

Whether or not you use a Project Planner with your letter proposal, your solution must be interesting, plausible, affordable, and well organized. The objectives should be summarized in such a manner that the funder can almost "see" the gap shrink between what is and what ought to be.

Your letter proposal should focus on one solution — the one with the greatest chance of matching the values of the prospective grantor. If you have done your homework, you know what they value and have described a need that will motivate them to agree that the area you are addressing is important. By this point in your proposal the prospective grantor should believe that the gap *must* be closed, and closed *now.* If this is the case, the funding source will not be able to put your proposal down until they have at least read your suggested solution.

It is, however, possible for them to disagree with your solution. Even if you did your homework, they may have values, feelings, and/or prejudices you did not know about. They could say that they don't think your solution will work, that they have already funded a grant that tried the same solution, or that there are other applicants with better or more interesting solutions. But if you are fortunate enough to still have their attention and they are interested in the potential benefits of the solution, the next item to be addressed in your letter proposal is cost.

5. REQUEST FOR FUNDS — HOW MUCH THE SOLUTION/PROJECT WILL COST

Grantors have limited funds. In fact, they receive many more proposals than they can fund. Estimates are that private funders grant only 10 percent of the requests they receive. Ultimately they must judge *which projects* produce *what benefits* for *how many* of the target population. The decision will ultimately be based on which grantee offers the most compelling benefits for the population the funder values.

State the amount you are requesting. If appropriate, divide the cost of the project by the number of students the project will serve. This will give you the cost per student served. Remember that your project has a "roll-out" or future benefit because each student served will go through life with more skills, better job opportunities, and so on. If your proposal deals with parent or teacher training, roll out your project's benefits to the number of individuals these trained people will come in contact with. When dealing with facilities and equipment, identify how many will utilize the resource over its lifetime. For example: "X number of families will utilize the Middlesex Recreational Facility for Y hours over a 10-year period." In an example like this, the cost per person served could be as little as pennies per hour, depending on the figures!

Multiple Funders — Obviously your letter proposal must state the amount you are requesting from the grantor you are sending the proposal to. However, if your project requires funding from more than one source, you should also let them know that you will be seeking additional funds from other corporations and/or foundations. Avoid saying, for example, that you hope to get funded by the Smith Corporation, the Jones Foundation, and so on. State the exact number of other funders being approached. Also cite grantors that have *already* agreed to partially fund your project. Present the total amount already received and the amount outstanding.

For jointly funded projects it is crucial that the grantors know that you are tailoring your proposal to each prospective funding source and that you have done your grants homework.

Some grantors may be justifiably concerned that their part of your project will get lost in the shuffle or that they will not receive appropriate credit. To alleviate these concerns, use a colored highlighter to visually separate each grantor's part of the total project on your project planner and refer each grantor to the Project Planner so that they can see how integral their portion is to the whole plan.

Matching Costs and In-Kind Contributions — Some grantors require that a portion of the project costs be borne by the grantee. While many federal grantors require matching contributions, several foundations and corporations also require grantees to pay for part of their projects. Even if a matching or in-kind contribution is not required, you may still want to include one to demonstrate your dedication to your goal. Private grantors are concerned that the organizations they fund be committed to supporting their projects after grant funds are depleted. By demonstrating your school's commitment in advance through a matching or in-kind contribution, you show that you have not applied for the grantor's money without carefully analyzing your own commitment. Designate matching and in-kind contributions on your Project Planner with an asterisk (*).

What to Do if the Grantor Requests a Budget — 32,000 of the 33,000 foundations probably will not require that you submit a budget with your letter proposal. Of the 1,000 who may, only a few hundred will request that a specific budget format be used.

If you have developed a Project Planner, preparing the budget will be a simple task. For a letter proposal budget, you will probably just have to provide a summary of the major line items on your Project Planner. However, be sure to let the grantor know that more detailed budget information is available upon request.

If no budget format is specified, present the budget in a paragraph or block form. Use a minimum of space and short columns instead of long ones. For example:

> We are requesting a grant of $20,000 from the Smith Foundation. To demonstrate our school's support of this important project we will provide $8,000 in matching support. A detailed budget is available upon request.

	Request	Match	Total
Salaries & Wages	$10,000		$10,000
Stipends/Teachers In-Service		$7,000	7,000
Consultants/Evaluation	3,000		3,000
Equipment/Lab	7,000		7,000
Printing/Materials		1,000	1,000
TOTAL	$20,000	$8,000	$28,000

6. UNIQUENESS — WHY YOUR SCHOOL SHOULD GET THE GRANT INSTEAD OF SOME OTHER SCHOOL

Since funding sources will be asking themselves this question anyway, why not bring it up yourself? Why *should* your school, classroom, or consortium get this grant? Couldn't another school initiate the methods and do the project just as well? The answer to the last question is no, for the following reasons.

- First, you developed the idea for the project! It is your baby.

- Second, you have documented your school's/classroom's need. The opportunity to act is where you are.
- Third, you developed the idea with the help of experts in curriculum development, evaluation, and so forth. You arranged for their input, gathered them together, and worked with them. In other words, you have already invested many, many hours developing a project that will be a successful model.

Brainstorm what positive forces are at work that can convince the grantor that your school is indeed the best school to fund. For instance, in addition to superior facilities, you may also have unique individuals whose commitment and expertise make your school the funding source's most logical choice. If you are to be the project director, put in a plug for yourself. For example, "Ms. Jane Doe [your name] is slated to direct the project. Ms. Doe has been recognized as an outstanding educator by the South Dakota Department of Education and has more than 12 years of experience in classroom teaching." You can say something good about yourself because you are not going to sign the letter. Yes, that's right. Although you may write many letter proposals, you will seldom be the person to sign them. In general, your letter proposal should be signed by the highest-ranking individual in your school system. So put in something complimentary about yourself. Then, when your top-ranking administrator signs it, it will become the truth!

7. Closing Paragraph — How to Conclude Your Letter Proposal

Use the closing paragraph to reaffirm your school's commitment to the project and to invite the funder to work with you on achieving the project's anticipated results. You should also reaffirm your willingness to provide the funding source with any additional materials that may help them make their decision. You could invite the grantor to visit your school or classroom to observe the needs firsthand.

Always include the name and phone number of your contact person in the closing paragraph. In many cases the individual whose signature appears on the proposal knows very little about the details of the project. You might say something like, "Please contact Jane Doe, the project director, at 716-358-4501 for proposal details."

8. Signatures — Who Should Sign the Proposal

Taking the grantor's point of view into consideration, ask yourself whose signature will have the greatest impact on the funding decision. In your case, it is most likely to be the signature of your superintendent or building principal, although some schools prefer to have proposals signed by the assistant superintendent for instruction, the business officer, or the curriculum specialist. Some proposals are submitted with two signatures — the president of the school board's and a top- ranking school administrator's. It may be appropriate to have several signatures on proposals that require special cooperation, collaboration, or coordination. For example, a consortium proposal may have the signatures of all the cooperating parties.

Attachments

Most foundations and corporations do not allow or encourage attachments. While attachments may help answer questions that arise when a proposal is being read, the problems they create for understaffed foundations and corporations often prohibit their inclusion.

What about pictures, videotapes, audiotapes, and slides? It certainly seems that in the age of electronics, these components would be allowed. However, even when you are dealing with manufacturers of electronic equipment, find out what is allowed before submitting your proposal. While electronic tools may be highly effective in preproposal contact, they may be useless during the actual proposal review. For example, what good would it be to submit a videotape with your proposal if the reviewer does not have access to a VCR?

What's in Store for the Future?

Foundations in some states are joining together to support a standard format for grant applications. However, it is not likely that this effort will bear fruit in the near future. If you follow the information and application guidelines in the various resource books, make preproposal contact when possible, and expand your network of informal links, you can be fairly certain that your proposal's format will be acceptable to your prospective funding source and that someone will read it.

Two sample letter proposals are included for your review — one to a foundation and one to a corporation (figs. 13.1 and 13.2).

SAMPLE LETTER PROPOSAL
TO A FOUNDATION

January 6, 1993

Ms. Elaine Finsterwald, Trustee
Smith Foundation
123 Money Place
Jonesboro, NC 28699

Dear Ms. Finsterwald:

The Smith Foundation is synonymous with the word *children*. Since 1927, your grants have provided creative solutions to the needs of young people in Jonesboro and our state. Your recent annual report highlights your commitment to children's early school years and to family involvement and responsibility in education. The $1.5 million in grants you have awarded over the past three years to strengthen children and their families clearly demonstrates your dedication and concern.

[You could mention previous support to your school district or the number of children who have been touched by any past support. For example, "Your grant to renovate an elementary classroom into the Smith Computer Lab has directly touched the lives of over 5,000 students in four years. Scores on standardized tests have improved 40 percent."

If the Smith Foundation has not funded elementary or middle school education directly, show how their support for your school-based project relates to their interest in programs related to the welfare of children, improving family life, parental responsibility and involvement, and so on.]

Previous generations have progressed through our schools with the involvement and encouragement of teachers and parents. Today, classroom leaders lacks much of the support they used to get from parents and must compete with television and video games for a child's time and attention.

How much time do children spend watching television versus doing homework? A study of 25,000 middle school children conducted by the Department of Education reported 21.4 hours per week of television versus 5.6 hours of homework (*Wall Street Journal,* March of 1992). When asked if parents placed limits on television, two-thirds of the parents surveyed said yes, while two-thirds of the children said no. These results suggest that some parents may have a problem setting priorities for their children.

Other results of the study point to the deterioration of parental responsibility and involvement in educational activities. For instance, four out of five parents surveyed reported that they regularly discuss schoolwork with their children, while two out of three children said parents rarely or never discuss schoolwork with them. Apparently the breakdown in communication between parents and children is at crisis proportions.

The need exists to develop and implement programs that encourage parents to become involved in their children's education. This means more than just visiting the school. For example, the Department of Education study also showed that 50 percent of parents had visited their child's school for meetings, but only 33 percent had visited their child's classroom.

What happens when parents take responsibility for working with their children and their children's school?

- Students whose parents discuss schoolwork with them get higher grades.
- Restrictions on television viewing tend to boost grades.

While some adults may think that the way to improve education is to increase funding for schools, taxpayers in Harrison, Arkansas, do not. While national test scores for students in Harrison rank in the top 10 percent of the country, Harrison ranks 272d out of Arkansas' 327 school districts in education taxes (*USA Today,* November 18, 1991). The key is parental involvement. Almost 100 parents volunteer for one hour a week at each of the town's elementary schools, and parents and teachers meet each year to establish education goals for the next year.

What can we do in Jonesboro to promote the sharing of responsibility for education among schools, parents, and children? Teachers, parents and students at the Jonesboro Elementary School have developed a program entitled Responsibility in Education through Academic Partners (REAP). The REAP program is aimed at increasing responsible educational behavior and encouraging parental involvement in the classroom and at home. Teachers will actually work with parents and students to develop tailored, individual contracts to produce increases in all levels of education and the quality of all course work.

The attached Project Planner outlines each objective and the activities that will foster the changes we desire. From increasing test scores to promoting public and volunteer service, the Jonesboro Elementary School will provide the catalyst through the education and involvement of parents in their children's responsible use of "out-of-school" time. The project is not limited to decreasing television viewing, but "TV Busters" are included in the plan.

We are requesting a grant from the Smith Foundation for $20,000 to initiate this project. Based upon our preliminary work with the teachers and Parent Advisory Committee of Jonesboro Elementary School, we anticipate the involvement of 600 students, 360 parents, and 40 teachers. Your grant funds will represent an investment of $20.00 per person served for the first year of the project. Future funding needs will be significantly less once the materials have been developed under your grant award. Our School District will provide $6,000 of in-kind contributions to support the project.

The Jonesboro Elementary School is fortunate to have Renee Weathers as the project director. Ms. Weathers was named the "1992 Outstanding Teacher of the Year" by the North Carolina State Education Department. She will be assisted by the Parents Advisory Committee, chaired by Sam Price. The Committee is supported by a group of 52 parents, who have already volunteered 200 hours to develop the REAP program and this proposal.

We believe that you REAP what you sow in life, and we invite you to "sow with us" by supporting Responsibility in Education through Academic Partners.

Jonesboro Elementary School's tax exempt status is __________, and our tax exempt number is __________. Renee Weathers is available at 200–861–4000 to answer your questions and to provide additional information that will help you arrive at your funding decision.

Sincerely,

Attachment

SAMPLE LETTER PROPOSAL
TO A CORPORATION

January 12, 1993

Clyde L. Baker
Contributions Officer
Widget Corporation
4321 Commercial Park
Rocker, NY 14570

Dear Mr. Baker:

John Allen, your marketing manager, advised me to contact you for consideration of a grant from Widget Corporation. John, who has volunteered over 100 hours to our Parents Advisory Committee, has told us of your company's interest in and efforts to promote responsible behavior in your employees and their families. It is with this common interest in mind that the Casper Elementary School requests a grant of $20,000 from the Widget Corporation for the Responsibility in Education through Academic Partners Program (REAP).

John Allen has been instrumental in guiding our school's curriculum group toward understanding the changes technological advances have brought to Widget Corporation and how these changes influence what types of employees and skills your corporation will require in the future.

Technological advances have also brought changes to the family. Everything from health to educational achievement to parent/child communication has been affected by television, videos, and computer games.

We have learned in education that *what* children devote their time to determines the skills they develop. Unfortunately, our children are devoting an inordinate amount of time to television. A study of 25,000 middle school children conducted by the Department of Education revealed that the children surveyed spent an average of 5.6 hours per week on homework and 21.4 hours per week watching television. In addition, when asked if parents placed limits on television, two-thirds of the parents surveyed said yes, while two-thirds of the children said no.

We are not suggesting that television viewing is inherently bad. However, the amount of television children watch is one possible indication of the responsibility parents take for their children's "out-of-school" time and ultimately for their education.

A parent's responsible involvement in his or her child's education can also be evaluated by the time spent discussing schoolwork within the family and the type or quality of parental contact with the child's school. The Department of Education's study revealed some disturbing facts in these areas as well.

- Four out of five parents surveyed reported that they regularly discussed schoolwork with their children, while two out of three children said they rarely or never discussed schoolwork with their parents.
- Fifty percent of the parents surveyed reported visiting their child's school for meetings, while only 33 percent had visited their child's classroom.

When you compare what can result from parental involvement and responsibility in education with what can result from a lack of parental involvement and responsibility in education, the problem is clear and the goal evident. Students whose parents discuss schoolwork with them get higher grades, and restrictions on television viewing tend to boost grades.

What can be done? This is the question that brought John Allen and over 100 other parents together to prepare a plan for action. The program they developed is entitled Responsibility in Education through Academic Partners (REAP).

REAP seeks to involve parents, students, and teachers in generating a monthly educational contract for change. Each signed contract is individually tailored and aimed at developing realistic and responsible educational behavior. Each contract outlines a plan to utilize "out-of-school" time more effectively.

The objectives of the project and the activities aimed at bringing about the desired changes are outlined on the enclosed Project Planner spreadsheet. The activities deal with involving parents and students in setting outcomes for education and presenting alternatives such as "TV Busters," a program initiated by a Minnesota teacher, to help kids break the television habit.

Developing the materials and initiating the program generate the project's major costs. Once established, REAP's volunteers and teachers will keep the program going. What is required now is a grant of $20,000 from Widget Corporation.

The Widget Corporation's support will directly affect the lives and education of 600 students, 360 parents, and 40 educators. Over a four-year period, this one-time grant represents an investment of $5.00 per person served. In fact, since the children that participate in the program will learn what can result from a responsible parental role in education, the benefits will accrue over many, many years.

The Widget Corporation's support will be recognized in the REAP program's informational brochure, and space will be set aside on the brochure's inside cover for a statement from Widget Corporation.

Alice Jones has been selected as the project director. She is eminently qualified and has worked with parents in this region for over twenty-five years. As a sign of commitment, the school district has agreed to provide support services valued at $6,000.

The volunteers have done all they can do. The time is right. Please join with us in sowing the seeds for responsible, parental involvement in education.

Money alone does not ensure a great education. Responsible commitment does. In Harrison, Arkansas, national test scores ranked among the top 10 percent in the country, while education taxes rank 272d out of Arkansas' 327 school districts. What's the key? *Parental Involvement.* Approximately 100 parents volunteer one hour per week at each of the town's elementary schools, and parents and teachers work together each year to determine the following year's educational goals.

This project is truly an investment in our community. Alice Jones is ready to provide any additional information you may need to make your funding decision. Please call her at 321–987–0645. Our school's tax exempt status is _______ and our tax exempt number is ___________.

Sincerely,

The research you have collected on your prospective funding source will show any deadline dates for submitting your proposal if there are any. Some grantors have no deadlines. Proposals are read periodically or as needed. If there is a deadline, submit your proposal slightly early. While this will eliminate the *need* for special delivery or express mail service, you may still want to send your proposal by one of these means so that you can obtain a signed receipt for delivery to assure you that your proposal made it to the right place.

However you decide to send your proposal, you should have a mock review before submission to increase your chances of funding. As with federal grants opportunities, you want to be sure you are submitting a proposal that embodies your best effort and reflects well on your school.

Organizing a Foundation/Corporate Proposal Improvement Group

Invite four or five individuals to form a group to help you improve your proposal prior to submission. Ask a variety of individuals to participate, including parents, students, educators, foundation/corporate board members, and anyone else you would like to involve in helping you develop your proposal. Note that a foundation or corporate board member can provide particularly valuable insight into the private grants review and decision-making process. Just be aware that once your volunteers realize how easy it is to develop a quality proposal for a foundation or corporation, they will want to take responsibility for more and more components of the proposal development process!

Mock reviews are much easier to perform for foundation and corporate proposals than for federal grant applications. First, it's fun to play the role of a wealthy and educated foundation or corporate board member. And second, it takes less time to read and make comments on foundation and corporate proposals than federal proposals because they are generally shorter.

Basically, you will be asking them the four of five individuals invited to participate in your proposal improvement group to meet to conduct a mock review of your proposal that will be as much as possible like the actual review.

In most cases, the group members will spend only five to ten minutes reviewing the proposal. The entire evaluation process will be completed in less than one hour. If you will be submitting your proposal to a large foundation that has a required format and hires experts to review proposals, ask your volunteers to review, comment on, and score your proposal before they meet as a group. The best way to find out about the review process of large corporations is to request the information in preproposal contact.

The Foundation/Corporate Proposal Improvement Scoring WorkSheet

Complete the Foundation/Corporate Proposal Improvement Scoring Worksheet (fig. 14.1) in advance of your group meeting. Eventually you will make a copy of the worksheet for each group participant and distribute the worksheets at the meeting.

Record any information you have been able to uncover on the worksheet. This includes, but is not limited to:

- who reads the proposals,
- how much time will be spent reviewing each proposal,
- the scoring system or criteria used for evaluation, and
- research on the grants history of the grantor.

Unfortunately, in most cases you will not have much information to record. Remember, private grant funds are not public money; therefore, private grantors are not required to provide you with information on the review process. In addition, most private grantors do not use an elaborate scoring or evaluation system.

What about background information on private funding officials? You can get some information from resource books such as *Who's Who* and *Standard and Poor's Register of Directors and Executives*. You should at least be able to provide your group members with the officials' ages and educational backgrounds and sometimes with brief biographies.

Give the volunteers a description of the funding source and any information you have on the types and numbers of proposals it has funded. If the funding source is a foundation, a copy of its IRS tax return will also help your group members. At the beginning of the meeting review the information to be sure the group members have a good idea of the grantor's point of view.

If you are in doubt about how much time the grantor spends reading each proposal, use a five-minute time limit. Even when your knowledge of the grantor is limited, a mock review is still an excellent investment of time when you consider the potential benefits.

Ask your volunteers to read the proposal quickly and to designate areas that they think will appeal to the grantor with a plus sign (+) and areas that need improvement with a minus sign (-). At the end of the five minutes, ask one volunteer to act as the recorder and to list the positive points on the worksheet. Ask the participants to briefly discuss the positive points and then to rank order them, starting with the most positive. Have them repeat this procedure for the negative points. Finally, ask the participants to list suggestions for improvement.

In order not to impede the group's free expression, it would be best if you left the room after naming the recorder. Don't worry — the rank ordering of the positive and negative areas will tell you how strongly the mock reviewers felt about specific parts of your proposal. This information plus the group's list of suggestions for improvement will give you valuable food for thought as you rewrite your proposal and put the finishing touches on your final version.

FOUNDATION/CORPORATE PROPOSAL
IMPROVEMENT SCORING WORKSHEET

The following information is being provided to help you review the attached foundation/corporate proposal.

The Proposal Will Be Read by:

________ funding official

________ funding staff

________ review committee

________ board members

________ other _______________________________________

Amount of Time Spent Reviewing Each Proposal:

Socio economic Background of Reviewer(s);

Known Biases or Viewpoints:

Past Grants to Education (including amount and recipient)

Positive Points   **Rank Order**

Negative Points   **Rank Order**

Other Comments/Suggestions for Improvement:

CHAPTER FIFTEEN

Dealing with the Decision, Follow-Up, and Building Your Grantseeking Base

The Decision

FEDERAL GRANTING AGENCIES

Rejected Proposal — When a proposal is rejected, a grantseeker's first reaction is to withdraw from grantseeking and go into hibernation. Okay, you worked hard and you did not win. But you must act proactively, as you did when you began the grants process. After all, you knew when you started that not everyone ends up a winner. Remember that even grantseekers who are successful 50 percent of the time fail the other 50 percent. There are not enough federal grant funds to support *all* of the *best* projects. You must now make a *rational* decision about whether you should resubmit your proposal. Review the following suggestions and keep your feelings in check.

Immediately send a thank-you letter to the federal agency official you have been in contact with. Thank the official for her help and let her know that you understand the agency's funding constraints. Ask to be sent your reviewers' comments and include a self-addressed label. Explain that your grants research indicated that the agency's program presented a great opportunity for funding because of its concern for your area of interest. Inform her that you will be contacting the agency in the near future concerning the next submission date and grants cycle. Ask the federal program official if she anticipates the availability of any unsolicited funds or if there is any chance that one of the successful applicants may not expend all of the granted monies in the time frame allowed. You could use any unexpended funds or unsolicited funding to do part of your project, which would make you a better applicant in the future.

Keep in contact with the funding source! Get ready for next year. Your chances may actually be better after you have been rejected because the reviewers' comments and insights will help you improve your proposal. Demonstrate a positive attitude and a sincere concern for the funder.

If you receive a letter that gives you a priority score and explains that you are not yet rejected but that the score is not adequate to attract funding, do not be a grants spoiler and protest your score. Do not take the rejection personally. React constructively and positively and do not burn any bridges or alienate any funders. If you resubmit, your proposal is supposed to be judged by a new panel of reviewers, which means that you have a new chance of being funded. Try to be objective and rational about the likelihood of your project being funded upon resubmittal. If your score was very low, ask the federal grantor if it would be best for you to develop a whole new approach.

Accepted Proposal — Many federal program officers who grant millions of dollars each year never receive thank-you letters or requests for reviewers' comments. (In many cases, applicants do not receive reviewers' comments unless they request this valuable feedback in writing.)

Be different. Send a thank-you letter and ask for the reviewers' comments. Include a self-addressed label. Remember, you need to know what you did that resulted in your high ranking so you can repeat the techniques. In addition, invite the granting officials to visit your school. They have the legal authority to make a site visit, but it looks better if you invite them.

FOUNDATION/CORPORATE GRANTORS

Rejected Proposal — The private grantor normally does not have the resources or support system necessary to provide you with your reviewers' comments and scores. Since private grant funds do not come from tax dollars, you have no right to this information. Since you probably will not receive much feedback, you may decide that it is best not to ask for it.

Send the foundation or corporation a thank-you letter. In your letter, tell them that you will reapply for funds unless they advise you not to. In the worst-case scenario, the grantor meets once a year. When they gather to review grant applications, they will find your thank-you letter from last year and a new request for this year. Tell them that you understand that they limit their staff so they can use their resources on grants instead of payroll. You will not lose anything by sincerely thanking them for their time and the opportunity to compete for their grant funds. You might even invite them to visit your school. But you must face the fact that some of your proposals will be rejected. Make the best of the situation. Be positive and resubmit.

Accepted Proposal — You may receive a phone call or a letter informing you of your good fortune. Some foundations meet so infrequently and have such a limited staff that you will actually receive a check for your full request *with* the notification of your award. Immediately send a thank-you letter. Invite the grantor to visit your school and ask if they would like a presentation made by your students, teachers, and/or parents or a short video on your project to show at a future board meeting. Request any comments they could provide on your proposal, including negative as well as positive feedback.

NONPROFIT ORGANIZATIONS AND ASSOCIATIONS

Rejected Proposal — When your request for a grant is denied by an association, a civic group, or a fraternal club, it is even more important to send a thank-you letter than it is with federal, foundation, or corporate grantors. You are likely to see these grantors in your school and community again and again. Say thank you and ask for suggestions for improvement and directions for resubmittal. Point out that the problem is not going to go away by itself and tell them that they will be hearing from you again. These funders interpret persistence as commitment, and you *are* a committed educator and community member.

Accepted Proposal — Voluntary organizations, service clubs, and fraternal groups like to keep their members and donors informed about educational changes they have supported. Send a thank-you letter to them immediately upon receiving word about your grant award and volunteer to make a presentation at their meeting or conference. Including your students in the presentation will make it even better.

Follow-Up

Federal Granting Agencies

Follow-up with federal granting agencies can be divided into two basic categories: contact with the funder *while* your proposal is being reviewed and contact with the funder *after* the proposal outcome has been announced.

Contacting the Federal Agency While Your Proposal Is Being Reviewed

— A federal agency will consider contact from you during the period between the deadline and notification of the outcome as an attempt to influence the review and scoring system. Therefore, when your proposal is in submission, you should contact the funder *only* on the rare occasion when you must forward information of major significance — for example, a new scientific breakthrough has been made that will allow you to cut the price of budgeted equipment drastically; or another grantor has partially funded the project and you want to reduce the amount of your request; or you need to withdraw the grant request. If you lack one of these three drastic reasons, stay away from the grantor while your proposal is being reviewed! This includes any intervention or contact by elected officials.

Contacting the Federal Agency After the Proposal Outcome Has Been Announced

— Unfortunately, many funding officials hear from prospective grantees only at the time of submittal. Actually, they should hear from grantees early in the funding cycle and again after the proposals have been reviewed. You are encouraged to contact the funder after your proposal outcome has been determined, whether your grant has been accepted or rejected.

Follow-up after acceptance is necessary to arrange the transfer of funds, site visits, and so on. How you will operate your grant depends on the system your district utilizes. It is crucial that you receive instructions on how to access your grant funds and that your record keeping and hiring and purchasing procedures comply with federal guidelines.

Most school districts have to deal with federal programs on an ongoing basis and therefore have all the necessary procedures in place. There are two basic transfer systems for providing grantees access to their federal grant monies. The first is for the grantee to provide a cash forecast to the federal granting agency and for the federal grantor to send the money in advance, based on the needs outlined in the forecast. In your case, funds would be sent to your school district *before* grant expenditures were made. In the second transfer system, the grantee pays all proposal expenses up front, and the federal grantor reimburses the grantee *after* the fact. In other words, your district would pay your proposal expenses up front, and the federal grantor would reimburse the district after the expenditures were made. In either case, you need to know who handles the funds in your district and how you can access them.

In addition, you should develop a system for keeping track of any reports required by the federal granting agency. You may have agreed to send them progress indicators, milestones, or products. Keep in contact, comply with report requirements and deadlines, and meet all of your responsibilities in a timely manner.

Foundation and Corporate Grantors

Follow-up with foundations and corporations that have no staff and rarely meet is very difficult. Even though private funding sources meet infrequently, mail them materials that point out or highlight their interests. Send pictures or news releases that demonstrate what you have accomplished with their funds and with the support of other funding sources.

Building Your Grantseeking Base

Continue to build your base of likely funders for your school and classroom projects. File your project ideas and useful news and research articles in your appropriate Grants Workbook (see chapter 2).

Keep up your webbing and linkage contacts. Stay alert for contacts that can provide access to granting officials. Once you get the ball rolling, the grants process will become more and more familiar to you and easier to control.

The biggest danger you will encounter in grantseeking is *success.* Success in grantseeking may distract you from your primary focus — teaching. If you do not mind being called from your classroom to assist other educators who want grantseeking information, you have nothing to worry about. But be forewarned. The concepts in this primer work. Use the suggested techniques and you will succeed. The funds you generate will increase your power and influence. But most important, the benefits to your students, your school, and your community will be phenomenal. Good luck!

Bibliography

Government Grant Resources

Commerce Business Daily

> The government's contracts publication, published five times a week, the *Daily* announces every government Request for Proposal (RFP) that exceeds $25,000 and upcoming sales of government surplus. **Price:** $261 annually or $130 for 6 months. **Order from:** Superintendent of Documents,U.S. Government Printing Office,Washington, DC 20402, 202-783-3238

Catalog of Federal Domestic Assistance (CFDA)

> This is the government's most complete listing of federal domestic assistance programs with details on eligibility, application procedures, and deadlines, including the location of state plans. It is published at the beginning of each fiscal year with supplementary updates during the year. Indexes are by agency program, function, popular name, applicant eligibility, and subject. It comes in looseleaf form, punched for a three-ring binder. **Price:** $46 annual subscription. **Order from:** Superintendent of Documents, U.S. Government Printing Office, Washington, DC 20402, 202-783-3238

The Federal Register

> Published five times a week (Monday through Friday), the *Register* supplies up-to-date information on federal assistance and supplements the *Catalog of Federal Domestic Assistance* (CFDA). It includes public regulations and legal notices issued by all federal agencies and presidential proclamations. Of particular importance are the proposed rules, final rules, and program deadlines. An index is published monthly. **Price:** $340 per year. **Order from:** Superintendent of Documents, U.S. Government Printing Office,Washington, DC 20402, 202-783-3238

United States Government Manual

> This paperback manual gives the names of key personnel, addresses, and telephone numbers for all agencies, departments, etc., that constitute the federal bureaucracy. **Price:** $23 per year. **Order from:** Superintendent of Documents, U.S. Government Printing Office, Washington, DC 20402, 202-783-3238

Academic Research Information System, Inc. (ARIS)

> ARIS provides timely information about grant and contract opportunities, including concise descriptions of guidelines and eligibility requirements, upcoming deadlines, identification of program resource persons, and new program policies for both government and nongovernment funding sources.

Biomedical Sciences Report	$210
Social and Natural Science Report	$210
Arts and Humanities Report	$125
All three ARIS Reports and Supplements	$495

Order from: Academic Research Information System, Inc., The Redstone Building, 2940 16th Street, Suite 314, San Francisco, CA 94103, 415-558-8133

1992 Federal Funding Guide

This guide describes programs that provide grants and/or loans to local, county, and state government, nonprofits, community, and volunteer groups. **Price:** $248 plus $12.50 postage and handling. **Order from:** Government Information Services, 1611 North Kent Street, Suite 508, Arlington, VA 22209, 703-528-1082

Federal Grants and Contracts Weekly

This weekly contains information on the latest Requests for Proposals (RFPs), contracting opportunities, and upcoming grants. Each ten-page issue includes details on RFPs, closing dates for grant programs, procurement-related news, and newly issued regulations. **Price:** $349 for 50 issues. **Order from:** Capitol Publications, Inc., 1101 King Street, PO Box 1453, Alexandria, VA 22313-2053, 800-327-7203

Health Grants and Contracts Weekly

Price: $320 for 50 issues. **Order from:** Capitol Publications, Inc., 1101 King Street, PO Box 1453, Alexandria, VA 22313-2053, 800-327-7203

Education Daily

Price: $537 for 250 issues. **Order from:** Capitol Publications, Inc., 1101 King Street, PO Box 1453, Alexandria, VA 22313-2053, 800-327-7203

Education Grants Alert

Price: $299 for 50 issues. **Order from:** Capitol Publications, Inc., 1101 King Street, PO Box 1453, Alexandria, VA 22313-2053, 800-327-7203

Washington Information Directory, 1992

This directory is divided into three categories: agencies of the executive branch, Congress, and private or "nongovernmental" organizations. Each entry includes the name, address, telephone number, and director of the organization and a short description of its work. **Price:** $72.95. **Order from:** Congressional Quarterly, Inc., 300 Raritan Center Parkway, Edison, NJ 08810, 1-800-638-1710

Foundation Grant Resources

Many of the following research aids can be found through the Foundation Center Cooperating Collections Network. If you wish to purchase any of the following Foundation Center publications, contact: The Foundation Center, 79 Fifth Avenue, Dept. ME, New York, NY 10003-3076, 800-424-9836. In NY State: 212-620-4230

Corporate Foundation Profiles, 7th edition, 1992

This Foundation Center publication contains detailed analyses of 250 of the largest corporate foundations in the United States. An appendix lists financial data on hundreds of additional corporations with assets of $1 million or that give at least $100,000 in grants every year. **Price:** $135. **Order from:** The Foundation Center

The Foundation 1,000

This research aid profiles the 1,000 largest U.S. foundations by foundation name, subject field, type of support, and geographic location. There is also an index that allows you to target grantmakers by the names of officers, staff, and trustees. **Price:** $195. **Order from:** The Foundation Center

The Foundation Directory, 1993 Edition

This is the most important single reference work available on grantmaking foundations in the United States. It includes information on foundations having assets of at least $2 million or annual grants exceeding $200,000. Each entry includes a description of giving interests, along with address, telephone numbers, current financial data, names of donors, and contact person, and IRS identification number. Includes six indexes: state and city, subject, foundation donors, trustees and administrators, and alphabetical foundation names. The trustees index is very valuable in developing linkages to decision makers. **Price:** $185 hardcover. $160 softcover. **Order from:** The Foundation Center

The Foundation Directory Supplement, 1993

The *Supplement* updates the 1993 edition of the *Directory* so that users will have the latest addresses, contacts, policy statements, application guidelines, and financial data. **Price:** $110. $275: hardcover *Directory* and *Supplement*. $250: softcover *Directory* and *Supplement*. **Order from:** The Foundation Center

The Foundation Directory Part 2, 1993 Edition

This *Directory* provides information on over 4,500 midsize foundations with grant programs between $50,000 and $200,000. Published biennially. **Price:** $160. $415: hardcover *Directory, Supplement, Part 2*. $390: softcover *Directory, Supplement, Part 2*. **Order from:** The Foundation Center

The Foundation Grants Index, 21st edition, 1993

This cumulative listing of over 55,000 grants of $5,000 or more made by over 800 major foundations is indexed by subject and geographic locations, by the names of recipient organizations, and by key words. **Price:** $125. **Order from:** The Foundation Center

Foundation Grants to Individuals, 8th Edition, 1993

Comprehensive listing of over 2,300 independent and corporate foundations that provide financial assistance to individuals. **Price:** $55. **Order from:** The Foundation Center

The National Guide to Funding for Elementary and Secondary Education, April 1993

Includes over 1,600 sources of funding for elementary and secondary education and over 4,500 grant descriptions listing the organizations that have successfully approached these funding sources. **Price:** $135. **Order from:** The Foundation Center

Education Grant Guides, 1992/1993 Editions

There are 7 Grant Guides in the field of education including: Elementary and Secondary Education, Higher Education, Libraries and Information Services, Literacy, Reading and Adult/Continuing Education, Scholarships, Student Aid and Loans, Science and Technology Programs, and Social and Political Science Programs. There are 23 other guides in areas other than education, such as children and youth, alcohol and drug abuse, minorities, etc. Each guide has a customized list of hundreds of recently awarded grants of $10,000 or more. Sources of funding are indexed by type of organization, subject focus, and geographic funding area. Price: $60 each **Order from:** The Foundation Center

Foundation News

Each bimonthly issue of the *News* covers the activities of private, company-sponsored, and community foundations, direct corporate giving, and government agencies and their programs, and includes the kinds of grants being awarded, overall trends, legal matters, regulatory actions, and other areas of common concern. **Price:** $29.50 annually or $53 for 2 years. **Order from:** Foundation News, PO Box 96043, Washington, DC 20077-7188, 301-853-6590

LRCW Newsbriefs (Lutheran Resources Commission Newswbriefs)
This monthly is geared to providers of human services and to anyone wanting to keep up-to-date on government grant deadlines. It is a 30-page bulletin of resource material for program development in over 28 subject areas as well as for resource development in general. **Price:** $70 per year. **Order from:** Lutheran Resource Commission, Woodward Bldg., Suite 900, 733 15th St., NW, Washington, DC 20005, 202-667-9844

The Taft Foundation Information System
Foundation Reporter: This annual directory of the largest private charitable foundations in the United States supplies descriptions and statistical analyses.

Foundation Giving Watch: This monthly publishes news and the "how-to's" of foundation giving, with a listing of recent grants.

Foundation Updates: This publication supplies new information on 100 foundations per year. **Price:** $443 (all three publications); $327 (*Foundation Reporter* only); $139 (Newsletter only, one year/12 issues). **Order from:** Taft Group, 835 Penobscot Building, Detroit, MI 48226, 800-877-8238

Education Funding News
This weekly report also provides funding information. **Price:** $239 for 50 issues. **Order from:** Government Information Service, 1611 N. Kent Street, Suite 508, Arlington,VA 22209, 703-528-1082

Foundation and Corporate Grants Alert
Price: $227 for 50 issues. **Order from:** Capitol Publications, Inc., 1101 King Street, PO Box 1453, Alexandria, VA 22313-2053, 800-327-7203

Private Foundation IRS Tax Returns
(Available from the IRS or free to use at Foundation Center)
The Internal Revenue Service requires private foundations to file income tax returns each year. Form 990-PF provides fiscal details on receipts and expenditures, compensation of officers, capital gains or losses, and other financial matters. Form 990-AR provides information on foundation managers, assets, and grants paid and/or committed for future payment. The IRS makes this information available on aperture cards that may be viewed at libraries operated by the Foundation Center or at its regional cooperating collections. You may also obtain this information by writing to the appropriate IRS office (see accompanying list). Enclose as much information about the foundation as possible, including its full name, street address with zip code, its employer identification number if available, and the year or years requested. It generally takes four to six weeks for the IRS to respond, and it will bill you for all charges, which vary depending on the office and number of pages involved.

INTERNAL REVENUE SERVICE CENTER REGIONAL OFFICES

Central Region (Indiana, Kentucky, Michigan, Ohio, West Virginia)
Public Affairs Officer, Internal Revenue Service Center, PO Box 1699, Cincinnati, OH 45201

Mid-Atlantic Region (District of Columbia, Maryland, Virginia, Pennsylvania — Zip Codes 150-168 and 172)

Public Affairs Officer, Internal Revenue Service Center, 11601 Roosevelt Blvd.,
Philadelphia, PA 19154

Midwest Region (Illinois, Iowa, Minnesota, Missouri, Montana, Nebraska, North Dakota, Oregon, South Dakota, Wisconsin)
Public Affairs Officer, Internal Revenue Service Center, PO Box 24551,
Kansas City, MO 64131

North Atlantic Region (Connecticut, Delaware, Maine, Massachusetts, New Hampshire, New York, New Jersey, Rhode Island, Vermont, Pennsylvania — Zip Codes 169-171 and 173-196)
Public Affairs Officer, Internal Revenue Service Center, PO Box 400,
Brookhaven, NY 11742

Southeast Region (Alabama, Arkansas, Georgia, Florida, Louisiana, Mississippi, North Carolina, South Carolina, Tennessee)
Public Affairs Officer, Internal Revenue Service Center, PO Box 47-421,
Doraville, GA 30362

Southwest Region (Arizona, Colorado, Kansas, New Mexico, Oklahoma, Texas, Utah, Wyoming)
Public Affairs Officer, Internal Revenue Service Center, PO Box 934,
Austin, TX 78767

Western Region (Alaska, California, Hawaii, Idaho, Nevada, Washington)
Public Affairs Officer, Internal Revenue Service Center, PO Box 12866,
Fresno, CA 93779

Corporate Grant Resources

Annual Survey of Corporate Contributions
This annual survey of corporate giving is sponsored by the Conference Board and the Council for Financial Aid to Education. It includes a detailed analysis of beneficiaries of corporate support but does not list individual firms and specific recipients. **Price:** $20 for Associates. $80 for Nonassociates. **Order from:** The Conference Board, 845 Third Avenue, New York, NY 10022, 212-759-0900

The National Directory of Corporate Giving, 2d Edition
This directory provides information on over 1,500 corporate foundations plus an additional 600 direct, corporate giving programs. It also has an extensive bibliography and six indexes to help you target funding prospects. **Price:** $195. **Order from:** The Foundation Center, 79 Fifth Avenue, Dept. ME, New York, NY 10003-3076, 800-424-9836. In NY State 212-620-4230

Directory of Corporate Affiliations
This directory lists divisions, subsidiaries, and affiliates of thousands of companies with addresses, telephone numbers, key persons, employees, etc. **Price:** $687 plus handling and delivery. **Order from:** Reed Reference Publishing, PO Box 31, New Providence, NJ 07974, 800-323-6772

Dun and Bradstreet's Million Dollar Directory, 5 volumes
The five volumes list names, addresses, employees, sales volume, and other pertinent data for 160,000 of America's largest businesses. **Price:** $1,310 for 5 volumes. **Order from:** Dun and Bradstreet Information Services, 3 Sylvan Way, Parsippany, NJ 07054, 800-526-0651

Standard and Poor's Register of Corporations, Directors and Executives
> This annual register provides up-to-date rosters of over 400,000 executives of the 46,000 nationally known corporations they represent, with their names, titles, and business affiliations. **Price:** $550 for one year, includes quarterly supplements. **Order from:** Standard and Poor's Corporation, 25 Broadway, 17th Floor, Attn: Sales, New York, NY 10004, 212-208-8786

Taft Corporate Giving Directory, 13th Edition, 1992
> This directory provides detailed entries on 589 company-sponsored foundations. Included are nine indexes. **Price:** $327 plus postage and handling. **Order from:** Taft Group, 838 Penobscot Building, Detroit, MI 48226, 800-877-8238

Corporate Giving Watch.
> This monthly reports on corporate giving developments. **Price:** $139 a year. $442 plus postage and handling for *Taft Corporate Giving Directory* and *Corporate Giving Watch.* **Order from:** Taft Group, 838 Penobscot Building, Detroit, MI 48226, 800-877-8238

Computer Research Services

Congressional Information Service Index (CIS Index)
> CIS covers congressional publications and legislation from 1970 to date. It covers hearings, committee prints, House and Senate reports and documents, special publications, Senate executive reports and documents, and public laws. It includes monthly abstracts and index volumes. Noncomputer grant-related materials are also available from CIS including a CIS *Federal Register* Index, which covers announcements from the *Federal Register* on a weekly basis. **Price:** $1,040 hardbound annual edition. Monthly service (including hardbound annual edition) is on a sliding scale ranging from $1,045 - $4,310, depending on your library's annual book, periodical, and microform budget. **Order from:** Congressional Information Services, Inc., 4520 East West Highway, Suite 800, Bethesda, MD 20814, 800-638-8380

DIALOG Information Services
> 3460 Hillview Avenue, Palo Alto, CA 94304, 800-3-DIALOG. A commercial organization that provides access to hundreds of databases in a range of subject areas. DIALOG has no start-up fees or monthly minimum charges, but there is an annual fee of $35. Foundation Center files cost $1.10 per minute to search on line. Each full record printed off line or by DIALOG costs an additional $.40.

Federal Assistance Program Retrieval System (FAPRS)
> The FAPRS list more than 1,250 federal grant programs, including planning and technical assistance. All states have FAPRS services available through state, county, and local agencies as well as through federal extension services. For further information, call 202-708-5126 or write to:
>
> 1. Your congressperson's office; they can request a search for you, in some cases at no charge.
>
> 2. Federal Domestic Assistance Catalog Staff, GSA/IRMS/WKU, 300 7th Street SW, Reporters Building, Room 101, Washington, DC 20407

Foundation Center Databases
> The Foundation Center offers the public two online computer databases — *The Foundation*

Directory file and *The Foundation Grants Index* file. Both databases are available online through DIALOG. The cost for this service is $95 for up to 75 records and $.50 for each additional record. **Contact:** The Foundation Center, 79 Fifth Avenue, New York, NY 10003-3076, 800-424-9836. In NY State 212-620-4230.

The Sponsored Programs Information Network (SPIN)

This is a database of federal and private funding sources. A microversion is available as well as online. **Price:** Online — $500 annually plus $10 per search or $3,500 annually with unlimited searches. Microversion — $2,995 for biweekly updates; $1,995 for monthly updates; $1,195 for quarterly updates; $695 for annual updates. **Order from:** InfoEd, 453 New Karner Rd., Albany, NY 12205, 518-464-0691